George Hugh Smith

A critical History of Modern English Jurisprudence

A Study in Logic, Politics, and Morality

George Hugh Smith

A critical History of Modern English Jurisprudence
A Study in Logic, Politics, and Morality

ISBN/EAN: 9783337076139

Printed in Europe, USA, Canada, Australia, Japan

Cover: Foto ©ninafisch / pixelio.de

More available books at **www.hansebooks.com**

A Critical History

OF

Modern English Jurisprudence

A STUDY IN LOGIC, POLITICS, AND

MORALITY

*Non a Prætoris edictu, neque a Duodecim Tabulis, sed
penitus ex intima philisophia haurienda
juris disciplina.*

BY

GEORGE H. SMITH

AUTHOR OF

"Right and Law," "The Law of Private Right," and Essays in the
American Law Review on "The Certainty of Law and the
Uncertainty of Judicial Decisions," "The True Method of
Legal Education," and other subjects.

SAN FRANCISCO
BACON PRINTING COMPANY
1893.

PREFACE.

A limited edition of this little work has been printed, with a view of submitting it to friends of the author, and others, who, he may have reason to suppose, are interested in political science. But in submitting it even to this limited class of readers, the author is painfully conscious, from experience, that both the subject of the work, and the method in which it is treated stand in need of apology.

In regard to the subject,—which is Jurisprudence,—its study in England and this country, within the last fifty years, has fallen into almost entire neglect; and there is now no subject more generally unpopular. The general reader regards it as belonging peculiarly to the province of the lawyer, and the lawyer, in general, as a study of no practical utility, and, with which, consequently, he has no concern. And the few who are addicted to philosophy, turning to the works of the modern English jurists, find there something which bears no resemblance to real Jurisprudence, but which has usurped its place, and even its name.

This so-called jurisprudence is the theory of Austin, (the principal subject of our review,) which has become so generally received and firmly established in English philosophy as to occupy exclusively the whole field of Jurisprudence. But this theory, as will be shown more fully in the body of the work, asserts, as its fundamental principle, that the law (*Jus*) is merely an expression of the arbitrary will of the government, or state; and, consequently, that rights, and Justice or Right, are the mere creatures of that will. Hence, if the theory be true, it follows that Jurisprudence,—which, as universally conceived by all but the modern English jurists, is the Science of Justice or Right,—can have no existence. There is nothing, therefore, to surprise us in the fact that the study of the subject has fallen into decay. For true Jurisprudence, so far as opinion can effect such a result, has been abolished in England and English-speaking countries; and the *pseudo* Jurisprudence that has been substituted for it, as may be verified by reference to the current works upon the subject, is, of all others, the dreariest and the most uninviting.

But real Jurisprudence, the science of Rights, or of Right or Justice, is, in fact, the science of the necessary conditions of rational social life, and therefore the fundamental part of Political and Social Philosophy. And, as of all the departments of the Science of Human Nature it is of most transcendent and vital importance, so it excels them all in the scientific rigor of its method,— which approaches nearly to that of Geometry,—and, consequently, in the certainty of its results. Hence, if we leave out of view its fortunes in England during the present century, no other branch of philosophy has had a grander history ; nor is there another that excels, or even equals it, either in the genius of those who have devoted themselves to its study, or in the interest and beneficence of the results achieved. For among its devotés, (or, as Celsus calls them in the passage cited below, its priests,)

"*Jus est ars boni et æqui*, of which some one deservedly calls us the priests ; for we conduct the cult or religion of Justice, and profess the knowledge of the Good and the Equal, separating the equitable from the inequitable, and distinguishing the lawful from the unlawful * * * following, if I am not deceived, a true, and not a spurious philosophy." Pandects II., 1, § 1.

are numbered all the great philosophers of the world, from Socrates, Plato and Aristotle, to Kant and his followers, inclusive ; and among its achievements, the development of the Roman Law, the reconstruction of political society in Europe, when emerging from the anarchy of the dark ages, and the institution of International Law or Right. In short, its history is the history of human civilization ;

for civilization itself, in the proper sense of the term, is merely the capacity of a people for social life, or, in other words, its capacity for realizing justice; and Jurisprudence may, therefore, without impropriety, be said to be the Science of Civilization.

From this science and its literature, consisting of the best work of the greatest intellects of the race, and to which in the continental countries of Europe fresh additions are being constantly made, English-speaking peoples, since the advent of Bentham and Austin, and by the predominance of their philosophy, have been effectually isolated; and it may, therefore, with confidence be asserted that no task can be nobler, or, to the philosophic mind, more interesting, than the one I have here, however inadequately, attempted; namely, to refute the fantastic and pernicious theory by which the English mind has been so long dominated, and by which, for the time being, it has been reduced, in its capacity to deal with jural and political science, to a state approaching imbecility, and to rehabilitate in our midst true Jurisprudence.

It remains to add a few words in explanation of the method in which the subject of the work is treated; which, with the average reader, it is to be feared, will prove equally unpopular as the subject itself. The modern English theory of Jurisprudence is universally admitted to be the creation of Austin; by whom the loose and popular notions of Bentham were reduced to a rigidly coherent system. But Austin himself, for his fundamental principles, drew largely upon Hobbes, whose philosophy is thus necessarily brought within the scope of our inquiries. The history of modern English Jurisprudence, therefore, consists, almost exclusively, of the works of Hobbes and Austin; and hence our investigations will, in the main, be confined to a review of their reasoning. Now, it happens that the works of Hobbes and Austin present the most striking and instructive examples anywhere presented,—and, in modern times, almost the only iv

examples,—of the application of the analytical or logical
method to political science; and, hence, an adequate review of their works will be scarcely less interesting as a
study in logic, than on account of their political theories.
And this aspect of the subject, for several reasons, will be
found peculiarly deserving of our attentions. For the
use of this method, which consists in the accurate formulation of our premises, and in reasoning rigorously from
proposition to proposition, as in geometry, presents, over
all others, at once a great advantage and a great danger.

For, on the one hand, it is its peculiar merit, if we regard
it as a means of discovering truth rather than as an instrument of persuasion, that the logical development of an
argument discloses its weak points, and thus, if the same
method be used in reviewing it, facilitates the detection of
error. And, hence, the mistakes of great reasoners, like
Hobbes and Austin, are always more apparent, or at least
are much more easily pointed out, than those of loose and
inconsequent thinkers. On the other hand, a logical
argument, if understood, forces assent, unless some error
or inaccuracy can be detected in the premises; and even an
argument only apparently logical will be equally persua-
sive until the fallacy lurking in it be discerned. But
where an argument is skillfully constructed, this task,
whether it be the detection of a fallacy in the reasoning,
or of a weakness in the premises, requires the closest and
most critical examination of every link in the chain of
reasoning. Hence, while the logical method facilitates the
detection of error, it is, to readers careless of their logic,—
as is, in fact, remarkably illustrated by the influence of
Hobbes' philosophy, and the domination of Austin's theory
over the English mind, — a most powerful instrument of
deception. The use of this method in our present investigations is, therefore, imperatively demanded, on the two-
fold ground that it is, at once, the readiest, and the only
adequate means by which error can be detected and refuted in the reasoning of such masters of the craft as
Hobbes and Austin.

But, independently of this consideration, there is another reason that imperatively demands our adoption of this method; for it is, in fact, the true method of political science, and the only one from which assured results can be anticipated; as is, in fact, demonstrated affirmatively by the example, not only of Hobbes and Austin, but also of Aristotle, Bacon, Locke, Hume, Grotius, and other great reasoners, and negatively, by the lack of convincing power in the great mass of the political, social, and moral disquisitions of the day. Hence, if we would justly weigh the reasoning of Hobbes and Austin, or even understand it, we must adopt their own method; and, in doing this, in addition to the knowledge we may otherwise gain, and which cannot in any other way be obtained, we will learn from their example the true and the only method for the successful investigation of the problems of jurisprudence and of political science generally; of which method it is one of the principal objects of this work to demonstrate the efficacy and power.

But the logical or analytical method demands the use of a style altogether different from that in common use,—which may be called the popular or rhetorical. For it is the peculiar characteristic of the logical style that it must be accurate or aphoristic, i. e., it must express the exact truth, without any admixture of error; for otherwise our conclusions will be altogether unreliable. And this requires the exact analysis of the meaning of the terms we use, and the formal statement of our propositions; which to the general reader is distasteful. For, while the logical style admits, and even requires, great brevity of expression,—so that in general the matter of volumes of ordinary popular disquisition may by means of it be compressed into a few chapters,—yet, it demands on the other hand, a degree of attention and independent thought, that only a few highly trained, or exceptionally gifted minds are willing to give, or, perhaps, are capable of giving.

The best type of this style is found in the mathematics,

1*

and especially in geometry, and also in the writings of the
classical jurists of the Roman law; and, at least in our
investigations, it can never be departed from without the
risk of error. Of the essential characteristics of this style
the writings of Hobbes and Austin are among the best examples; the former, on the whole, superior; but the latter, in their analytical parts, though lacking the graces
of rhetoric, excelling all others in a rigid observance of
the requirements of logic.

My own style I have sought equally to adapt to the
subject, and to the nature of our investigations, and I trust
I may say of it, without vanity, with Hobbes, that while
"there is nothing I distrust more than my elocution, nevertheless, I am confident, excepting the mischances of the
press, it is not obscure."

Los Angeles, June 11, 1893.

TABLE OF CONTENTS.

CHAPTER I.

INTRODUCTORY.

CHAPTER II.

HOBBES' THEORY OF JURISPRUDENCE.

CHAPTER III.

REVIEW OF HOBBES' THEORY.

CHAPTER IV.

THE BENTHAM-AUSTIN, OR LEGAL THEORY OF JURISPRUDENCE.

4

CHAPTER V.

THE RECENT ENGLISH JURISTS.

CHAPTER VI.

REVIEW OF THE AUSTIN THEORY OF JURISPRUDENCE.

CHAPTER VII.

OF UTILITARIANISM.

CHAPTER VIII.

OF THE TRUE NATURE OF RIGHTS AND OF THE LAW.

CHAPTER I.

INTRODUCTORY.

§ 1. The fundamental problem of political science is to determine the nature and extent of human rights; but this problem relates to three several subjects, which, though intimately connected, require separate consideration. These are the rights or powers of the State, the rights of individuals, and the law; which last is the means by which rights, public and private, are realized.

Strangely enough, this branch of political science,—supremely important as it is, — is, in our language, at the present time, without a distinctive name, generally recognized as belonging to it. The reason of which is, that the term, jurisprudence, the name really appropriate to it, and by which alone it can be adequately expressed, has been wrested from its true meaning by Austin and his followers, for the purpose of denoting certain varying and ill-defined notions of their own; and the conception originally denoted by it is thus left without a term to express it. We must, therefore, begin by restoring the term to its proper meaning.

The subject has been examined with care by Mr. Holland, and, though his conclusions appear to me to be erroneous, his views upon it present the question involved with great clearness, and may, therefore, be referred to with advantage. Jurisprudence, he says, is merely the knowledge of *jus*: but it happens that the latter term denotes, "not merely the sum total of laws, but also the sum total of rights, (*jura, rechte, droits,*) and the sum total of all that is just, (*justum, recht, droit*)"; and hence jurisprudence, accordingly as we use the term, *jus*, may denote "the science of any one of three things, viz: (1) of law, (2) of rights, (3) of justice." These several senses of the term he regards as essentially different, and hence is of the opinion that one of them must be adopted to the exclusion of the others.

Accordingly, he adopts the first of the definitions referred to, and regards it as a piece of good fortune that when we thus define jurisprudence, viz, as "the science

2

of law," we are spared the ambiguities which beset the
expression of that proposition in Latin, German, and
French, and which, in his opinion, have greatly obscured
its exposition in those languages.[1] In this Mr. Holland

[1] Jur. 12, 13.

agrees with Austin, and others of the modern English
school of jurists, all of whom regard the ambiguity of
the term, *jus*, *droit*, *recht*, etc., used in other languages
to denote the law, as a fruitful source of confusion and
inaccuracy of thought; and there is, perhaps, no other
point on which the English jurists so pride themselves
as on their supposed superiority in this respect to their
continental brethren.

Nor is there any other with reference to which the
vanity of their pretentions is more apparent; for while
there is, no doubt, a certain difference in the several
senses of the term jurisprudence, referred to by Mr.
Holland, yet it is equally certain,—as will be more fully
shown in the sequel,—that, in whichever sense it be used,
the term expresses, under certain modifications, the same
essential idea.

Thus if,—as we are admittedly at liberty to do, provided we consistently adhere to the definition,—we define
jurisprudence as the science of rights, it follows that it
is also the science of justice; for justice is but the observance of rights, or the rendering to every man his
right.

But, according to a conception almost universal, and
which will be explained more fully hereafter, the law itself is but the practical means of realizing rights; and,
if this conception be true, the term jurisprudence may
also be used, without impropriety, as in fact the lawyers
habitually use it, to denote the science or methodized
knowledge of the law of private right. For this branch
of the law is made up of the doctrine of rights, as recognized in the law, (or, in other words, of *actionable*, or
juridical rights,) and of the doctrine of actions; which
are but the forms or *formulæ* used for the enforcement
of rights, (or, as defined by Heineccius, *medium jus persequendi*); and, hence, if jurisprudence be regarded as
the science of rights, or of justice, the subject of private
right, or *justice* as actually administered by the courts,
must be regarded as belonging to it.

It appears, then, that of the three meanings of the term
jurisprudence, distinguished by Mr. Holland, the first and

second are identical; **and** that the **third** is entirely consistent with these, provided it be assumed, (as it is one of the principal purposes of this work to establish,) that the rights with which the law deals, are in fact, as they are in name, *rights*, in the proper **sense** of the term.

On this assumption, therefore, jurisprudence may be defined to be the science or doctrine of rights, or of justice or right; and may be regarded as theoretical or practical, accordingly as we have in view the abstract theory of rights, or the doctrine of rights as actually realized in the community by means of the law, or in other words, juridical rights.

With regard to the former, perhaps the best illustration of its scope and methods in recent English literature is presented by the political works of Mr. Herbert Spencer, and especially the "Social Statics" and "Justice"; both of which—the former preferably, and the latter with equal propriety—might have been entitled, "Jurisprudence." Of the latter, or practical jurisprudence, the best models are presented by the works of the classical jurists of the Roman Law, and those of the modern civilians, and especially Savigny; and also by the works of Grotius, and other writers on the Law of Nations and of Nature.[1]

This view of the nature of jurisprudence, though repudiated by the modern English jurists, and consequently, since the time of Austin, somewhat obsolete with us, is by no means a novel one; it is, in fact, the orthodox view of the subject, in which jurists generally, from the time of Aristotle, have, with the exception of Austin and his

[1]In this connection the following observations of Leibnitz on the Roman lawyers will be found interesting:

"I have often said,—observes that great jurist and philosopher,—that, after the writings of the geometricians, there exists nothing which in point of strength, subtlety and depth, can be compared to the works of the Roman lawyers; and, as it would be scarcely possible from intrinsic evidence to distinguish a demonstration of Euclid's from one of Archimedes or Apollonius, (the style of each of them appearing no less uniform than if reason herself were speaking through her organs,) so also the Roman lawyers all resemble each other like twin brothers; inasmuch, from the style alone of any particular opinion or argument, hardly any conjecture could be formed about its author; nor are the traces of a refined and deeply meditated system of natural jurisprudence anywhere to be found more visible or in greater abundance. And even in those cases where its principles are departed from, in compliance with the language consecrated by technical forms, or in consequence of new statutes or of ancient traditions, the conclusions which the assumed hypothesis renders it necessary to incorporate with the external dictates of right reason are deduced with a soundness of logic and with an ingenuity that excites admiration. Nor are these deviations from the law of nature so frequent as is commonly supposed." Cited by Dugald Stewart, Philosophy of the Human Mind, 2, 3, 3.

followers, substantially concurred. This, for the present, will sufficiently appear by reference to the definitions in the Institutions and Pandects of Justinian, given in the note, from which the definitions in the text are taken. Of the introductory parts of these works, the modern English jurists, from Austin down, are wont to speak with contemptuous severity; but, in fact, they may be taken as the best expression extant,—in brief space,—of the true nature and general principles of the law; and as such they have been generally accepted by continental jurists, and, until lately, by the jurists of our own law.[1]

§ 2. Thus defined, jurisprudence, as has been intimated, may be regarded as treating of, (1) the Theory of the State, (2) the Theory of Private Rights, and (3) the Theory of the Law.

The several problems thus presented by jurisprudence have given rise to many conflicting theories; and these—bearing as they do upon the most vital questions of practical politics, and imperatively demanding, in the opinions of their advocates, a realization in practice—have naturally aroused the strongest passions and prejudices of mankind. But, fortunately, or unfortunately, there is one country in which for a while all conflict seems to have ceased, namely, England; where of late years one theory has become so predominant—at least among theorists—as practically to exclude all others, and to be regarded, like the Copernican theory of the universe, or the doctrine of evolution, as no longer within the pale of legitimate discussion.

This theory, briefly stated, is that the power, or right of the State over its subjects is, from its essential nature, necessarily unlimited or absolute; that the law is but an expression, and rights and obligations but the creatures, of the sovereign will; and, consequently, that in that will alone is to be found the standard of the just and of the unjust. From this it follows, and the theory, in fact, asserts, that the notions of natural right or justice and of natural

---

[1] "*Justitia*, (i. e. the virtue,) *est constans et perpetua voluntas jus suum cuique tribuendi.*" Hence abstract, or, as it is called by Aristotle, *political* justice, consists in rendering to every man his right (*jus suum cuique tribuere*).

*Jurisprudentia est * * * justi atque injusti scientia;* and hence, it is said : *Præcepta juris sunt honeste vivere, alterum non laedere, suum cuique tribuere.*

Jurisprudence, or rather *jus*, (the law) is also defined by Celsus, as "the art of the good and equal" (*ars boni et æqui*); and he asserts—and, as I will endeavor to show, truly—that it is "a true, and not a pretended philosophy."

rights are mere **delusions** ; of which to speak seriously (to use an illustration of Sir Henry Maine) is as though one **were** to assert the Ptolemaic theory of the **heavens, or to** pretend to listen **to the music of** the spheres.

Of this doctrine, **as** originally conceived by Bentham, and as subsequently developed into a complete and **coher**ent system **by** Austin, and **of the** modifications it has **re**ceived at the hands of later writers, I propose **to give a** brief history, **and, at** the **same time, to** subject **it to a** critical examination. But there **are** several other **theories,** one directly opposed to this, and the others **intimately** connected with it, which, in order that the questions involved **may** be distinctly presented, must also be considered.

§ 3. Of these, the first to be mentioned is involved in the popular conception **of** rights ; which, **as** usually happens in such matters, has been adopted **by the law**yers, **and thus** become an integral part of the **common law**.

According to **this** doctrine,—of **which the** modern English theory is on every point the direct negation,—rights, **or at** least certain rights, exist naturally, and are, therefore, not the creatures but the cause of the existence of government; which, in **fact, owes its** origin **to the** necessity of securing their observance, **and** in advanced **societies** can exist only upon **the condition of** substantially securing them. Hence the necessity of establishing justice, **or** securing **the observance** of rights, **as it is** the cause (or *raison d'être*) and the condition of **government,** is also the measure of its power. That **this is the doctrine** of our law will **not** perhaps **be** generally conceded, **but** that it is so will sufficiently **appear in** the progress of our investigations.

§ 4. In the construction of their theory Bentham **and Austin** availed themselves largely of the reasoning of Hobbes ; **and hence the** theory **of** the former is commonly regarded as in substance a development **of that of the** latter; but, in fact, the two theories differ radically on the most essential points.

The points in which they agree are in **the** psychological theory that men are not susceptible **of** any other than self-regarding motives, and in the doctrine of absolute sovereignty ; but, with regard to the nature of rights, and of the law, they differ entirely,—Hobbes, on these points, as will be seen, **agreeing** substantially with the Common

Law doctrine, and Bentham and Austin inventing a theory altogether new. It will be necessary, therefore, on this account, as well as on account of its intrinsic interest, to examine at length the philosophy of Hobbes.

§ 5. The theory of the State asserted by Hobbes and Austin, and now generally prevailing in England, though in the peculiar form it there assumes not elsewhere accepted, is, in its fundamental character, identical with the modern doctrine of sovereignty as commonly held on the continent. The difference between the two is that the English theory rests upon an attempted demonstration, and has been logically developed to its ultimate consequences, and thus become a coherent system. But this is not the case with the more general doctrine of sovereignty, which, as commonly held, is scarcely more than a vague opinion, assumed without any attempt to demonstrate it, and without a clear perception of the consequences logically deducible from it.

But it is in this form that political theories are most formidable; for when a theory is logically developed its weak points are made apparent, and often the very attempt to demonstrate it will, by way of *reductio ad absurdum*, show its falsity. But a mere opinion until thus tested may, and generally does, vary in meaning, according to the varying temper of the mind and the exigencies of argument, and thus becomes an instrument by which the most opposite conclusions may be proved,—as, for example, is notably illustrated by the different uses made of the doctrine of a social contract by Hobbes, Locke and Rousseau, respectively. It will be necessary, therefore, before entering upon the consideration of the English theory of the State, to make a few observations upon the doctrine of sovereignty, with the view of justifying the assertion that as commonly held it is a mere unverified opinion, which cannot be sustained otherwise than on the reasoning of Hobbes, Austin and other English writers; and which, therefore, if sustained, must take the form in which it is asserted by the English jurists, and be regarded merely as an undeveloped form of their theory.

The term, sovereign, means simply, superior.[1] In a political sense, it denotes merely the monarch, or other supreme officer, or organization in the state; and its correlative, *sovereignty*, the power vested in the sover-

[1] Low Latin, *Superanus*, formed with suffix, *anus* from Latin *super*, "above." Skeat.

eign, whether consisting of one or many. Both terms are strictly comparative, and there is nothing in their original meaning to imply that the sovereign or supreme power in the state is absolute or unlimited.

Originally the terms were applied to the form of sovereignty at one time almost universally prevailing in Europe, which was that of a monarch or single sovereign ; but with the development of improved forms of political organization, their application has been extended to other forms of government, and the term sovereignty has thus come to denote the supreme political power of a state wherever vested. But obviously, in its original application to a single sovereign, it denoted a single thing, or unit, namely, the power of a single man, which was necessarily indivisible ; and this notion it has carried with it in its new application to a multiplex sovereign. Hence, sovereignty, whether vested in a single monarch, or in several different officers, or classes of officers, or in different departments, or, even, as in federal governments, in different states, is habitually conceived to be a single indivisible power ; and thus a problem of great difficulty presents itself, to the great bewilderment of political theorists, namely, the problem of determining where, in each particular case, the sovereignty is vested,—a task similar to that of locating an ignis-fatuus or will-o'-the-wisp, and which in fact, as we shall see, admits of as many varying solutions as the fancy may dictate. But however the problem is solved, or wherever the sovereignty be regarded as located, it is generally agreed that it is in its nature unlimited and absolute, as well as indivisible. " In all forms of government," says Blackstone,—in a passage often quoted, and which voices an opinion almost universal,—" there is, and must be, * * * a supreme, irresistible, absolute, uncontrollable authority, in which the *jura summi imperii*, or the right of sovereignty, exists."[1]

The genesis of this theory is readily accounted for by the historical events out of which it grew. In the struggle between the kingly power and that of the feudal lords, in the Middle Ages, the former naturally came to be regarded as the last refuge of personal security, and the only hope of organized social life ; and out of this arose an almost universal sentiment in its favor, which found its expression in the modern doctrine of sovereignty ; and this doctrine, either in its original form, as

[1] 1 Com. 48-9.

applied to a single monarch, or, in a secondary sense, as applied to other forms of government, has come to be so generally received in the political philosophy of Europe, that the term itself, in popular use, carries with it the connotation of being an absolute, despotic power, or right. And this notion, intensified by the events of the great English Civil War, and of the French Revolution, continues to prevail in Europe, and especially in England, and also to a considerable extent in this country.

Thus, the term *sovereignty* has come to be, what is called, a question-begging term. For, as commonly used, it assumes the theory connoted by it ; and argument in support of it becomes superfluous, and against it impossible. For, when an opinion rests upon the false sense of a term, it will not be affected by the refutation of any reasoning that may be urged in its support, but will survive, though every conceivable argument in its favor be shown to be untenable,—in this respect, the opposite seeming to take place from what occurs, under analogous circumstances, in the vegetable kingdom ; where, if the roots of a plant be destroyed, it will die ; but an opinion rooted in a general prejudice, though the reasoning upon which it rests be refuted, will seem for a while to seek, and apparently to find new roots, and a renewed life.

It may however be safely assumed, that, if there are any arguments in favor of the doctrine of absolute sovereignty, they have not escaped the unrivalled acuteness and penetration of Hobbes and Austin ; and that it must therefore stand or fall with the reasoning adduced by them in support of it.

CHAPTER II.

§ 1. All men are more or less blinded by prejudice and passion; and impartiality or indifference to the result of our reasoning is the rarest of all logical qualifications. On this account allowance must always be made, as in astronomy, for the "personal equation;" which is much more readily done in the case of the astronomer, whose mind is generally indifferent to the result, and the personal error therefore regular, than in the science of human nature, where nearly every problem excites the prejudices and passions of the mind and heart; and where, in general, the theory is first formed, and the reasoning to support it afterward sought, and the wish is often the father to the thought.

In the case of Hobbes, this correction is readily made. He lived during the struggle between the King and Parliament in England, and was profoundly impressed, both by experience and observation, with the misery occasioned by civil war. And this impression was probably exaggerated by congenital disposition; for it is related of him that he was brought prematurely into the world through his mother's fright at rumors of the coming of the Spanish Armada. From this, and the associations of his life, he was naturally led to espouse the royal cause, and it cannot be doubted that his theory was thus largely influenced. His works were composed at an advanced age, long after his political views had been formed, and, from the circumstances under which they were written, as well as from internal evidence, are obviously to be regarded rather as a political polemic in support of a preconceived conclusion, than as an impartial investigation of the political problem. Hence, while all the resources of his powerful and methodical genius are brought to the support of his thesis, there is much in his works that it would be difficult to believe represented his convictions, were we not familiar in our own times with the force of political prejudice.

But the task of making proper allowance for these

misleading influences is, in the case of men of Hobbes' logical turn of mind, immensely simplified by their general accuracy of thought and expression, which facilitates the detection of error. And it also usually happens, and notably so in the case of Hobbes, that writers of this character, in the more abstract parts of their work, where prejudice has less place to operate, themselves furnish us with the means of correcting their errors. Hence, the value of a philosophical work is not to be estimated by its success or failure in establishing completely the main thesis to which it is devoted, for in this respect nearly all have failed; but by the partial, and often undervalued results obtained, and chiefly by the more or less logical character of the method of reasoning observed. The main excellence of thought is clearness and precision; to be intelligently and clearly right is the greatest achievement, but it is no mean achievement to be logical, even in error; and, in fact, such errors have been the means by which philosophy has advanced. Thus it happens that incomparably the most valuable contributions to political philosophy in modern times are the works of Hobbes and Austin. For, though their conclusions are often false and paradoxical, they have at least taught, by actual example, the true method applicable to the science of jurisprudence, and the only method that can be looked to for any further progress in it.[1]

§ 2. The theory of Hobbes may be stated in the following propositions, which are classified accordingly as they relate to the theory of the state, of rights, or of the law.[2]

Of the State.

The fundamental assumptions of Hobbes' philosophy are the denial of moral distinctions, as naturally existing, and of the possibility of any motive of human conduct

[1] "When Leibnitz, in the beginning of the eighteenth century, reviewed the moral writers of modern times," says Mackintosh in his dissertation on the Progress of Ethical Philosophy, "his penetrating eye saw only two who were capable of reducing morals and jurisprudence to a science. So great an enterprise might have been executed by the deep, searching genius of Hobbes, if he had not set out from evil principles; or by the judgment and learning of the incomparable Grotius, if his powers had not been scattered over many subjects, and his mind distracted by the cares of an agitated life."

[2] Our citations are to the Leviathan, in the edition of Mr. Morley, published by George Routledge & Sons, London, Glasgow, and New York, 1887.

other than a regard to self-interest.[1] From the conflict thus necessarily arising between the desires of men, i. e , upon the assumed hypothesis of an absence of all moral restraint, they become enemies; and, in the absence of government, there results a state of never-ending war of every man against every man, in which condition "the notions of right and wrong, just and unjust, have no place. * * * Force and fraud are, in war, the cardinal virtues."[2]

But, from this condition, means of escape are presented, consisting partly in the passions, such as fear of death, desire of commodious living, etc., and partly in the reason, which suggests certain articles of agreement called "the laws of nature," but which are improperly so called, being, in fact, merely dictates of reason.[3] "The first and fundamental law of nature" is that men ought to endeavor to secure peace; and from this "is derived the second law, that a man be willing, when others are so too, * * * to lay down his right to all things, and be contented with so much liberty against other men as he would allow other men against himself."[4] And from this law a third follows, that men perform their covenants; for otherwise the condition of war will still continue.[5] In this (the third) law, "consisteth the fountain and original of justice"; which is defined to be the "keeping of covenants"; and injustice, to be "the not performance of covenant." But Hobbes here falls into an inconsistency,— adding that "whatsoever is not unjust is just." Hence,— as we shall see is asserted infra,— where there is no covenant there can be no breach, and therefore everything is just; which is inconsistent with the definition that justice is the "keeping of covenant."[6]

But, in the absence of government, covenants are invalid, because there is no security for their performance, "and therefore he who performeth first does but betray himself to his enemy; contrary to the right, he can never abandon, of defending his life and means of living."[7]

Hence "before the names of just and unjust can have place, there must be some coercive power to compel men equally to the performance of their covenants, by the terror of some punishment, greater than the benefit they expect by the breach of their covenant;" in the absence of

[1]Leviathan, 32, 33.   [4]Id. 66.   [6]Id. 72, 73.
[2]Id. 65.   [5]Id. 71.   [7]Id. 69, 72.
[3]Id. 66.

which "all men have a right to all things," and "nothing is unjust,"[1] but "every man will and may lawfully rely on his own strength and art for caution against all other men."[2]

The only way to erect such a coercive power, and thus to escape from the natural condition of war, is for men "to confer all their power and strength upon one man, or upon one assembly of men, that may reduce all their wills, by plurality of voices, into one will * * * This is more than consent or concord; it is a real unity of them all, in one and the same person, made by covenant of every man with every man; * * * This done, the multitude, so united in one person, is called a commonwealth; in Latin, *civitas*. This is the generation of that great "Leviathan," or, rather, to speak more reverently, of that "mortal God," to which we owe, under the immortal God, our peace and defence."[3]

The sovereign is created not by covenant between himself and the people, but by covenant of the people only, "one to another," and consequently there can be no breach of covenant on the part of the sovereign.[4] A covenant between the sovereign and the people may indeed exist, but it is inoperative, "for want of a superior power to enforce it."[5]

All men are equally bound by this covenant of society: he who consents, by his covenant; and he who does not, because, unless his consent be assumed, he is "left in the condition of war he was before, wherein he (may), without injustice, be destroyed."[6]

The sovereign power is, necessarily, indivisible. "For powers divided mutually destroy each other."[7] And the disposal of the succession is also necessarily in the existing sovereign. For, if not, then on his death "is the commonwealth dissolved, and the right is in him that can get it."[8]

Of the Nature of Rights.

"Right consisteth in the liberty to do or forbear;" "for nothing is signified by the word 'right' than that liberty which every man has to use his natural faculties according to right reason."[9]

[1]Id. 72. [4]Id. 85. [7]Id. 93.
[2]Id. 82. [5]Id. 85, 86. [8]Id. 93.
[3]Id. 84. [6]Id. 86. [9]Id. 66.

" The right of **nature**," or "*jus naturale*," consists " in
the liberty each man hath to use his own power as he will
himself for the preservation of his own nature * * *
and consequently of doing anything which, in his own
judgment and reason, he shall conceive to be the aptest
means thereunto." Hence, "every man hath a right to
everything, even to another's body."[1]

In a state of political society, this **natural right is limited** by the law **or** expressed **will of** the **sovereign, and**
"the liberty of **the** subject lieth, therefore, only **in those**
things which, in regulating their actions, **the sovereign**
hath pretermitted, such as the liberty to buy and **sell, and**
otherwise contract, etc.";[2] but, " in all kinds **of actions**
by the law pretermitted, men have the liberty," (or right)
"of doing what their own reason shall suggest for the
most profitable to themselves."[3] Hence, " Right," (*i. e.*,
rights in the aggregate) "is **that** liberty which the law
leaveth us."[4]

Of the Nature of the Law.

There is some inconsistency, **or at** least apparent inconsistency, in the views of Hobbes as to the nature of the
law, arising from the ambiguity of that term; which is
sometimes used to denote a statute, or **aggregate** of statutes (*lex*), and sometimes to denote *the law,* (or *jus*).
The two views will, therefore, **require a** separate statement.

The first is thus expressed :

"The civil law is, to every subject, those **rules which
the** commonwealth has commanded him, by **words, writ-**
ing, or other sufficient signs **of** the will, to make use of
for the distinction of right and wrong ; that is to **say, of**
what is contrary, and what is not contrary to the **rule.**"[5]

Here the term law is obviously used in the sense of *lex*,
which Hobbes expressly opposes to the term *jus*. " For,"
as he says, "right is liberty, namely, that liberty which
the civil law leaves us; but civil law is an obligation,
and takes from us the liberty which he **law of** nature
gives us. Nature gave a right **to** every man to secure
himself by **his** own strength, and **to** invade a suspected
neighbor by **way** of prevention; but the civil law takes

[1] Id. 65, 66.
[2] Id. 101.
[3] Id.
[4] De Corpore Politico. B. 2, Ch. 10, Sec. 5.
[5] Lev. 123.

away that liberty in all cases where the protection of the law may be safely stayed; for insomuch *lex* and *jus* are as different as obligation and liberty."[1] Or, as expressed in another work: "The names *jus* and *lex*, that is right and law, are often confounded; yet scarcely are there two words of more contrary effect; for right is that liberty which the law leaveth us, and law is that restraint by which we mutually agree to abridge one another's liberty."[2]

According to this view, it would follow that the courts would have to be regarded as dealing principally with matters outside of the law; for the principal function of courts of civil jurisdiction is to enforce rights; and the principles by which the courts are governed in doing so constitute a part, and indeed the principal part, of what the Romans called *jus*, and what we,—but, in Hobbes' view, improperly,—call the law; which includes not only *jus*, or right, in the strict sense, but also *lex*. But, according to another and more deliberate view of Hobbes, the law of nature, which is but another name for natural right, or justice, is part of the civil law of every state; and it is the function of the judge to administer it as he would any other part of the law. Thus regarded, therefore, the law is no longer opposed to, but includes *jus* or right. Here, it is obvious, the term civil law is used in the sense of the Latin *jus*, or in the sense of *droit*, *recht*, *derecho*, &c., in other languages; or, in other words, it would seem that Hobbes himself falls into the usage which he has elsewhere reprobated. And this he in fact does, though, as we shall see, he attempts to reconcile the inconsistency of the two propositions.

On this point, more on account of the intrinsic interest, and value of his views on the nature of the law, than on account of the argument, which will be found to be manifestly untenable, I quote, somewhat at more length than usual, his own language:

"The law of nature and the civil law contain each other, and are of equal extent. For the laws of nature, which consist of equity, justice, gratitude, and other moral virtues on these depending, in the condition of mere nature, as I have said before, * * * are not properly laws, but qualities that dispose men to peace and obedience. When a commonwealth is once settled, then

[1] Id. 134.
[2] *De Corpore Politico*, B. 2, Ch. 10, Sec. 5.

are they actually laws, and not before, *as being then the commands of the commonwealth, and, therefore, also civil laws.* For, it is the sovereign power that obliges men to obey; for, in the differences of private men, to declare what is equity, what is justice, and what is moral virtue, and to make them binding, there is need of the ordinances of sovereign power and punishment, to be ordained for such as shall break them; *which ordinances are, therefore, a part of the civil law.*"

"The law of nature, therefore, is a part of the civil law in all commonwealths of the world. Reciprocally also, the civil law is a part of the dictates of nature. For justice,—that is to say performance of covenant, and giving to every man his own,—is a dictate of nature. But every subject in a commonwealth hath covenanted to obey the civil law." "Civil and natural laws are, therefore, not different kinds, but different parts of law; whereof one part, being written, is called civil; the other, unwritten, natural.[1]

" A law that obliges all the subjects * * * that is not written, or otherwise published in such places as they may take notice of, * * * is a law of nature. * * * The laws of nature need not any publishing or proclamation." But, " the law of nature excepted; it belongeth to the essence of all other laws, to be made known to every man that shall be obliged to obey them * * * For the will of another cannot be understood, but by his own word or act, or by conjecture taken from his scope and purpose, which, in the person of the commonwealth, *is to be supposed* always consonant to equity and reason."[2]

" The interpretation of the law of nature is the sentence of the judge constituted by the sovereign authority to hear and determine such controversies as depend thereon, and consisteth in the application of the law to the present case. For, in the act of judicature the judge doth no more but consider whether the demand of the party be consonant to natural reason and equity; and the sentence he giveth is, therefore, the interpretation of the law of nature; which interpretation is authentic, because he giveth it by authority of the sovereign, whereby it becomes the sovereign's sentence, which is law for that time for the parties pleading."[3]

[1] Id. 124.
[2] Id. 126.
[3] Id. 128.

" But, because there is no judge, subordinate nor sovereign, but may err in a judgment of equity, if, afterwards, in another like case, he finds it more consonant to equity to give a contrary sentence, he is obliged to do it. No man's error becomes his own law, nor obliges him to persist in it. Neither, for the same reason, becomes it a law to other judges, though sworn to follow it. For, though a wrong sentence given by authority of the sovereign, if he know and allow it, in such laws as are mutable, be a constitution of a new law in cases in which every little circumstance is the same, yet in laws immutable, such as are the laws of nature, they are not laws to the same, or other judges, in like cases forever after. Princes succeed one another; and one judge passeth, another cometh; nay, heaven and earth shall pass; but not one tittle of the law of nature shall pass, for it is the eternal law of God. Therefore, all the sentences of precedent judges that have ever been cannot, all together, make a law contrary to natural equity; nor any example of former judges can warrant an unreasonable sentence, or discharge the present judge of studying what is equity, in the case he is to judge, from the principles of his own natural reason."[1]

[1] Id. 128, 129

CHAPTER III.

§ 3. The several points of Hobbes' argument, on the theory of the State, are summed up in the following propositions :

(1) "That the condition of mere nature, that is to say of absolute liberty, such as is theirs that neither are sovereigns nor subjects, is anarchy and the condition of war."

(2) "That the precepts by which men are guided to avoid that condition are the laws of nature."

(3) "That a commonwealth without sovereign power is but a word without substance, and cannot stand ;" and,

(4) "That subjects owe to sovereigns simple obedience."[1]

To these propositions, taken in their ordinary and proper sense, but little objection can be made ; but they are not the conclusions which Hobbes set out to prove, and which he would have us believe. They present, therefore, as will be seen, a clear case of irrelevant conclusion, or *ignoratio elenchi.*

Thus, the first proposition, slightly qualified, may be taken as substantially correct, but it cannot be accepted as a necessary consequence from principles of human nature ; nor can the argument upon which it is rested by Hobbes, namely, that man is incapable of any other motive than a regard to his own interest, be admitted. For a regard to the just claims, and even the welfare of others, or, in other words, justice and benevolence, or love, though less strong, are as clearly principles of human nature as selfishness. All that can be admitted on this point is, that with men in general the last is the predominating motive, and, with a great many, overrides all

---

[1]Lev. 162. To the last clause, *i. e.,* that "subjects owe to sovereigns simple obedience," is added, in the original, the qualification, "in all things wherein their obedience is not repugnant to the laws of God ", but I have omitted this, as being one of the cases to which I have referred, where Hobbes says what he obviously does not mean. For the passage is immediately followed by an argument to show that there are no cases in which the law of God justifies disobedience to the sovereign. (Id. 166, 167.)

3

others. Hence, taking men as we know them, the want of government must result in a state of conflict, which may very fairly be described as a state of actual, or ever impending war; and historically this conclusion, though in degrees varying with the grade of civilization, is fully verified. The proposition may therefore be assumed, not as necessarily true, but as an empirical generalization from past experience; and in this form it is a sufficient support for what Hobbes calls his first and second laws of nature; namely, that men should seek peace, and to that end subject themselves to government; propositions indeed that few dispute.

The third proposition, properly construed, is also obviously true, and is indeed involved in the preceding. For sovereign power, in its proper sense, is but the power of the government, whether it be greater or less; and the latter, therefore, cannot exist without the former. But this is far from being all of Hobbes' meaning. For, in his view, sovereign power is unlimited or absolute, and is also indivisible; and these are, therefore, the conclusions intended.

With regard to the first of these, it is sufficiently manifest that the power of government must be great; and we may even say with our author, *Non est super terram potestas quæ comparetur ei;* but that it is, or should be, either unlimited or irresponsible, or that it should be any greater, within the limits of our power to restrict it, than necessary for the efficient performance of its functions, does not follow from the premises; nor is there anything in the argument tending to establish such a conclusion.

With regard to the proposition that the sovereign power is indivisible, this necessarily follows, if it be admitted that it is unlimited. For, as is well argued by Hobbes, every division of the sovereignty necessarily impairs or diminishes it, or, in other words, limits it. For, leaving out of view the convenient fiction which regards the sovereign as one person, or, in other words, as a corporation or body politic, it is obvious that in complex or constitutional governments the power of every officer or department of the government is limited by that of others; and hence the notion of the divisibility of the sovereign power is inconsistent with the proposition that it is absolute. But this should be taken as a *reductio ad absurdum*, rather than as proof of the doctrine of absolute sovereignty. For, in fact, history abounds with examples of the actual division of the sovereign power ; as, for instance, in the past, the English and the Roman constitutions; and, in the present, our own constitutions, state and federal.

With regard to the fourth and last proposition, namely, **that** subjects owe to sovereigns simple obedience, this, if **it** be construed according to Hobbes' own definitions, may be readily admitted. For, according to the argument urged in support of it, *duty* is but the fear of evil consequences to be inflicted by the sovereign for disobedience, and it must therefore be admitted that, precisely to the extent there is ground for such fear, the duty, *ex vi termini,* must exist. Nor is anything added to the proposition by the supposition of a covenant upon the part of the sub-ject ; for covenants themselves are binding only so far as evil consequences to the individual **are** to be apprehended from their violation ; and " justice, **that is** to say, not keeping of covenants, is " itself **but** " a rule of reason by which we are forbidden to do anything destructive to our life."

But here Hobbes is inconsistent; **for** obviously **he** in-tends us to understand the proposition as asserting the existence **of** such duty upon the subject, in the sense in which men commonly use the term. But thus construed the proposition cannot, under his theory, **be** admitted ; for one of his fundamental postulates is that there is **no** such thing as duty in this sense. Hence, here, the prin-cipal object of Hobbes fails,—which was to inculcate, as it were, a religious reverence **for** " that Mortal God," Le-viathan, " to which we owe * * * our peace **and de-**fense." For his conclusion, construed according to **his** own theory, and rendered into plain language, **is** merely that men will generally find it to their interest to obey the Sovereign. Hence, according to his theory, the condition of man is **not** essentially altered by the institution of gov-ernment. **No** man **is** under any obligation to obey the government any further than his own interest, **as** under-stood by him, may demand ; but every man still " has a right to everything; even to one another's body," so far as the right can be exercised with impunity. He may rightly defraud and rob his neighbor, and secretly disobey Leviathan himself, provided he may think it conducive to his interest to do so ; for his right " of doing everything, which in his own judgment and reason he shall conceive to be the aptest means thereto," is modified merely by the fear of hurt from Leviathan. Hence, on Hobbes' theory, the natural state of war would still continue, modified merely by fear of the sovereign; from which would result merely a change of the weapons commonly used, namely, from open force to cunning, and secret fraud.

It is, therefore, obvious that Hobbes' argument is inconclusive, and with this we might dismiss it; but there is a certain element of error underlying the whole subject, consisting in the ambiguity of the term *power* or *sovereign power*, which, as we shall see, has misled Austin and later English writers, and from which Hobbes himself has not altogether escaped; and which must therefore be explained.

The term *power*, in its strict and proper sense, denotes *might*, or *actual power*. It is also commonly used to denote *rightful power* or *right*, or, in other words, the power which, according to right, one ought to have; as when we say that the owner of property has the power to dispose of it, or that the child is subject to the power of the parent. In this sense Puffendorf uses the term when he says, "power is that by which a man is enabled to do a thing lawfully";[1] and Rutherford, when he says, "Civil power is in its nature a limited power";[2] or when he says, "Right and moral power are expressions of like import";[3] and Leibnitz, when he says that right is moral power, and obligation, moral necessity."[4]

Hence, the proposition that the power of the sovereign is unlimited, may mean either that it has unlimited actual power, which is, in effect, to say that its power is unsusceptible of actual limitation, (for otherwise the proposition would not be universally true,) or that it has an unlimited right to dispose of the lives and fortunes of its subjects.

Hobbes, in the original statement of the problem to be investigated, does not fall into the error of confounding these two meanings of the term. For the problem as stated by him is to determine "what are the 'rights' and 'just' power, or authority of a sovereign."[5] And this obviously is the only sense in which the question is worthy of consideration. For, whether the actual power of gov-

[1] Bk. 1, Ch. 1, Sec. 19.
[2] 2 Inst. of Nat. Law, 393.
[3] Inst. of Nat. Law, B. 1, C. 1, Sec. 3.
[4] "*Est autem jus quædam potentia moralis, et obligatio, necessitas moralis. Moralem autem intelligo, quæ apud virum bonum æquipollet naturali, nam ut præclare jurisconsultus Romanus ait, quæ contra bonos mores sunt ea nec facere nec posse credendum est.*" Opera 4, 3, 294.
[5] Lev., Introduction.

ernment is limited or unlimited is purely a historical question, which can be answered only in one way, namely, by saying that, in fact, it always has been, in various degrees, limited. Hobbes' proposition is, therefore, to be understood as asserting the unlimited and irresponsible right or just power of the sovereign over its subjects ; and it becomes essential, therefore, in order to understand its significance, to bear in mind what he means by the terms *right* and *just*. For these, as we have seen, are used by him in a sense different from that in which they are commonly understood, and the proposition in fact means something quite other than what it appears to express.

As used by Hobbes, the term *right* signifies merely the absence of restraint imposed by law. The proposition, therefore, merely asserts that the liberty or power of a sovereign is not limited by law, regarded as the expressed will of the sovereign, (or *lex*); which is but to assert the truism equally applicable to the sovereign and to others, that a man's liberty or power is not limited by his own will.

The same result also follows if we consider the term *just*, as used in the phrase, "just authority." "The definition of justice," he says, "is no other than the not performance of contract, and whatsoever is not unjust is just." The authority of the sovereign is not unjust, because it is not limited by covenant ; and, therefore, it is just. The whole proposition, therefore, simply means that the sovereign power is not limited, either by positive enactment, or by contract; for, as we have seen, according to Hobbes' theory, the covenant by which the sovereign is created is exclusively between subjects, and the sovereign is not a party to it; and, if the sovereign make a covenant with a subject, it is void, for want of a superior power to enforce it.

But in the last proposition Hobbes forgets the reasoning upon which the proposition, that covenants between parties in a state of nature are void, was established by him; for the argument is merely that no man in a state of nature is bound by his covenant because he has no guaranty of performance by the other party. But this can have no application to the sovereign who has, in his own power, full guaranty of the performance of contracts made with his subjects.

When, therefore, Hobbes speaks of the right of the sovereign, he means something quite different from what is usually meant by the term; and, having due regard to the propriety of language, it is clear that the so-called right of the sovereign is not, in fact, a right, but a mere unbridled power.

From what has been said, the fundamental defect of Hobbes' theory is clearly apparent. It rests upon the negative assumption—the old thesis of the sophists—that, independently of human institution, there are no such things as moral distinctions, no right and wrong, no just and unjust, no rights or obligations; and this will be found to be the common fundamental assumption of Bentham and Austin, and the later writers of their school, and to be, in fact, the foundation upon which the modern English theory of the state rests. Whether this assumption be true or false, it is, in fact, the fundamental problem of political philosophy, and will hereafter be fully considered.

§ 2. One of the most valuable features of Hobbes' theory is what may be called his jural method, which consists in the view taken of the fundamental problem or problems which it is the aim of jurisprudence to solve; or, in other words, of the scope of the science.[1]

In Hobbes' view, as we have seen, a right consists in liberty to act, and rights in the aggregate, or *right*, in the general liberty which a man has to act freely.

But the term *right* contains in its signification another element, namely, the quality of rightness; and hence, the liberty which constitutes the right is not to be understood as actual liberty, but as just or rightful, or, as it may be more appropriately termed, *jural liberty*.

In this connection the term *power* is so far synonymous with liberty that it may be used indifferently in the definition. For these two terms differ merely as the words "may" and "can," and therefore combine in their signification the same essential ideas, namely, absence of restraint and ability to act; and while each denotes one of these notions, it also connotes the other. A right, therefore, may be defined as consisting in the jural liberty or power to act, (*facultas agendi*) in a particular case or class of cases. Rights, therefore, are but particular parts or divisions of the general liberty to which a man is rightfully entitled, and in the aggregate constitute such

---

[1] I have elsewhere attempted to explain the nature and scope of jurisprudence (Right and Law, Ch. v., Callaghan & Co., Chicago); and as the view there taken is substantially that of Hobbes, I here make use of it, in an abbreviated form, in explaining his theory.

liberty; and the ultimate problem of jurisprudence, regarded as the science of rights, is to determine the extent of the rightful or jural liberty of the individual.

But, obviously, such liberty exists in every case in which one may not rightfully be restrained by other individuals or by the state; and as, in general, this liberty exists, and as there is always a presumption in its favor, the immediate problem is to determine the exceptional cases in which it may be rightfully restrained.

But the rightful power or liberty to restrain the free action of another where it exists, like the power or liberty to do any other act, is, *ex vi termini*, a right ; hence, it follows that the liberty of the individual is limited, and limited only, by the rights of other individuals, or of the state.

It is precisely thus that the problem was conceived by Hobbes ; and accordingly, as we have seen, the question to which his attention was chiefly directed was to determine "what are the *rights* and *just power* or authority of a sovereign" ; but, as he did not conceive of the existence of moral distinctions independently of human institution, he lacked one essential element for the successful solution of the problem.

Hence, his paradoxical conclusion that in the state of nature every man has a right to everything, even to his neighbor's person ; which, if propriety of language be regarded, is obviously absurd. For the term, *right*, as universally conceived, implies an exclusive liberty ; and it is. therefore, as impossible for two rights to conflict, as for two bodies to occupy the same space at the same time.

Hence, also, he is forced to conclude that in a state of nature property could not exist ; though clearly a man is born at least with a property in his own person ; and the natural right of self-ownership is indisputable. And from this, as has been shown, with admirable acuteness and penetration by Herbert Spencer, all other rights can be logically derived. Naturally, therefore, he altogether failed to establish his theory, and in order to make an apparent solution was compelled to invent a fictitious social compact, and a fictitious mortal God.

Nevertheless, his conception of the fundamental problem involved, and of the mode of dealing with it, is profound, original, and true ; and his failure resulted simply from the omission of an essential element in the problem ;

28

which, as will be shown, if taken into account, renders it susceptible of an easy solution.[1]

§ 3. Hobbes' theory of the law is based upon his conception of the nature of rights, and his resulting conception of the method of jurisprudence, as explained in the last section. According to this view, a man's liberty or right prior to the institution of government is unlimited, but after the institution of government is limited by law. This limitation, however, does not in any way alter the essential nature of the right. It still consists in the natural liberty which every man has, within the limits imposed by the rights of other individuals, or the state, to govern his own life and actions according to his own reason. His liberty is less extended, but within its extent it is the same liberty that in a state of nature would constitute his natural right. Hence, the rights of a man in a state of political society, being merely the remainder of his natural right still left to him by the law, are of natural origin ; or, in other words, are natural rights. Nor can the sovereign himself create a right of any other kind, for whatever right he may confer upon a subject has its virtue and force from the right conferred upon the sovereign by the law of nature, and is, therefore, as much a natural right as the right of a man to property, sold or given him by another.

But rights constitute a principal topic of the law, and hence, the principles by which rights are determined constitute part of the law of the land, and as such are administered by the judges. Hence, as asserted by Hobbes, "the law of nature"—which is but another name for natural right—"is part of the civil law in all commonwealths of the world." Thus it will be perceived Hobbes' conclusions are directly the opposite of the two principal tenets of the modern English jurists, namely, that in fact there are no natural rights, and that the law of nature, or natural right, is not part of the law.

The proposition that the law of nature, or natural right, is part of the law of the land, is logically deduced by Hobbes from his premises, and presents his deliberate and controlling opinion upon the subject. But, as we have observed, it is in conflict with the definition of the law,

[1]The method of Hobbes is in fact identical with that of Herbert Spencer, and also with that of Kant ; by whom, indeed Mr. Spencer admits that he was anticipated, as Kant himself was by Hobbes ; though the conception was undoubtedly original with Mr. Spencer, who was unacquainted with the views of his predecessors.

as consisting of the commands of the sovereign; and the arguments used by him to reconcile the two positions are calculated to obscure his real view. These arguments are, substantially, that on the institution of government the law of nature becomes part of the civil law, as being then the command of the sovereign, who is always to be supposed to intend what is consonant with equity and reason. But, as we have seen, he elsewhere asserts, and with great force, that it is not in the power of the sovereign to abrogate the laws of nature; though, of course, he may violate them.[1] Obviously, therefore, the argument is based upon what is called a legal fiction; which may be described as an assumption recognized to be in fact untrue, made for the purpose of apparently reconciling conflicting positions.

There is also another argument of the same kind, by which our author undertakes to explain the fact that custom is part of the law, and which is as follows:

"When long use obtaineth the authority of a law, it is not the length of time that maketh the authority, but the will of the Sovereign signified by his silence; for silence is sometimes an argument of consent, and it is no longer a law than the Sovereign shall consent therein."[2]

But here Hobbes trips in his logic, and is guilty of the fallacy of an *undistributed middle*. His conclusion, obviously, should be that *sometimes* custom derives its validity from the will of the Sovereign, signified by his silence; which is obviously the case where the Sovereign, knowing of the custom, and deliberately considering it, permits it to continue, and not otherwise; for the maxim, "*qui tacet consentire videtur*," can have no application to the silence of a person who knows nothing of the matter. But, obviously, this argument also was invented merely for the purpose of logically reconciling an obvious fact with his definition of the law, as being a command of the Sovereign. Otherwise, it was unnecessary; for custom is clearly part of the law on obvious principles of natural reason.

But these peculiar views of Hobbes' do not constitute an essential part of his theory of the law; which, indeed, will be better expressed if they be stricken out,—to use an expression of the lawyers,—as *surplusage*. Thus amended, his views may be accepted as a true and accurate description of the law, and as one of the most valu-

[1] Ante, page 20.　　　　[2] Lev., 124.

able contributions that have been made to jural science; and also as one which, in fact, constitutes a great step towards the successful performance of the task to which, in the opinion of Leibnitz, he alone, or Grotius, was equal, —namely, the task of " reducing morals and jurisprudence to a science." But unfortunately, as we proceed, we shall have occasion to verify, in his case, the sad expression of Mark Anthony:

" The evil that men do lives after them,
The good is oft interred with their bones."

CHAPTER IV.

OF THE THEORY OF BENTHAM AND AUSTIN.[1]

§ 1. Bentham and Austin agree substantially with Hobbes in assuming, as a first principle, the proposition that men are not susceptible of any other than merely self-regarding motives, and also in the conclusion that the power of the sovereign is necessarily absolute. Hence, their theory on this branch of the subject may be regarded as substantially a reproduction of his, and it will be sufficient for our purpose merely to explain the points of difference.

The first principle of Bentham differs in form of expression from that of Hobbes, and, perhaps, regarded merely as a psychological theory, may be distinguished from it, but in its bearing on the theory of the state, its effect is the same. Briefly, it is as follows :[2]

"The will cannot be influenced except by motives; but, when we speak of motives we speak of pleasures and pains. * * * * * Nature has placed men under the governance of two sovereign masters, pain and pleasure. * * * The principle of utility subjects everything to these two motives."

Utility is defined as "the property or tendency of a thing to prevent some evil or to procure some good. Evil is pain, or the cause of pain. Good is pleasure, or the cause of pleasure." * * *

"He who adopts the principle of utility esteems virtue to be good only on account of the pleasures which result from it; he regards vice as being an evil only on account of the pains it produces." "Virtue is a sacrifice of a less interest to a greater, of a momentary to a durable, of a doubtful to a certain interest. Every idea of virtue that is not derived from this notion is as obscure in conception as it is precarious in motive. * * * * *Sic præsentibus*

---

[1] The subject of this chapter has been treated in the work already cited, "Right and Law"; but, as the matter is essential to the argument here, repetition to some extent is unavoidable.

[2] The citations, for the sake of brevity, are confined to Bentham's "Theory of Legislation," London, Trübner & Co., 1871, etc., and, unless otherwise noted, will be found in the first chapter

utare voluptatibus ut futuris non noceas. So use present pleasures as not to lessen those which are to come."[1]

Obviously, so far as the argument is concerned, the psychological principles of Bentham are identical with those of Hobbes, and the observations made as to the sufficiency of Hobbes' argument are equally applicable here; that is to say, it is clear, should the principle be assumed, that the necessity of government would be even more apparent than, in view of the actual constitution of human nature, it in fact is; but it would also follow that there would be no duty or obligation upon any one, any further than he might be impelled by the fear of punishment, to observe the will of the government; or upon the part of the government to regard the interest or welfare of his subjects; or, upon any man towards his neighbor, either to benefit him, or to refrain from injuring him; and finally, that Hobbes' state of never-ending war would still exist, with the difference only that, to the warfare of every one against his neighbor, would be added the warfare of Leviathan against him, and of him against Leviathan; and that fraud would thus, in general, be substituted for force. This indeed is, unfortunately, a substantially fair, though somewhat strongly expressed, description of the actual condition of modern civilization; but nothing surely could have a stronger tendency to aggravate it than the general acceptance of a theory that in effect asserts, not only the morality, but the necessity of such a condition.

From such premises it is obviously impossible to derive the notion of duty, either to the state or to our neighbors; and hence, as we have observed, Hobbes was compelled to invent the fiction of a social compact, and thus, by deliberate self-delusion, to reach the conclusion at which he

[1] In the above and numerous other passages, Bentham leaves no room for mistake as to his meaning; and it is one of the curiosities of literature that Mr. Mill should charge Dr. Whewell (whose works always seem to have excited in him a most unphilosophical animosity) with misrepresentation, for attributing to Bentham the proposition that "the test of morality is the greatest happiness of the agent himself." The "standard," Mr. Mill says, "is not the agent's own greatest happiness, but the greatest amount of happiness altogether." "Nor did he (Bentham) ever dream of defining morality to be the self interest of the agent." (Dissertations and Discussions, New York, Henry Holt & Co., 1882, Vol. III, pp 315, 162.) But this, if language is capable of expressing any idea unequivocally, is precisely what is asserted by Bentham; and accordingly Mr. Sedgwick (Encyc. Brit., Article, "Ethics"), after remarking that "a supreme and unquestioning self-devotion, in which all personal calculations are suppressed," is a distinguishing feature of Mill's own theory, justly observes that such "a phenomenon * * * in Bentham's view is not even possible."

aimed. But Bentham, while justly reprobating this artifice, adopts a method hardly less reprehensible, and, by taking advantage of the ambiguity of the term utility, introduces a new principle, essentially different from the one first assumed; namely, the principle of *general* utility, which is that the welfare or interest of men in general, and not that of the agent, is the test or standard of right. But this principle, though perhaps not true, at least asserts the reality of duty, and of the distinction between right and wrong,—of which the theory of private or individual utility is the direct negation; and hence the two theories are essentially distinct, and,—except upon one hypothesis, to be referred to hereafter,—irreconcilable.

Having thus changed his premises, Bentham proceeds easily enough to the remaining propositions of his theory, viz: that " the public good ought to be the object of the legislator "; which, as an abstract proposition, is true enough, but is open to the objection that, according to the theory, no motive can be conceived why the legislator should govern himself accordingly; for, even if the principle of general utility be assumed, the theory of Bentham admits of no possible motive to secure its observance, except so far as self-interest may be effectual for that purpose.[1]

Austin's theory agrees with Bentham's, except that he postulates the existence of a God, in whose will is to be found the ultimate standard of right; from whose known benevolence, it is to be inferred that the principle of general utility, or the welfare of mankind, is enjoined; and from whose power, and the consequent fear of punishment, it is also to be inferred that it is the interest, and therefore, *ex vi termini*, the duty of all men to observe his will. In this way the inconsistency between the theories of *individual* and of *general* utility is reconciled. But it is held by Austin that the will of God is not sufficiently known to us, either by revelation, or by the principle of general utility,—" which, he says, as an index to the divine will, is obviously insufficient,"—to serve as a practical standard; and that the will of the government must therefore be adopted for that purpose. Hence he concludes, with Hobbes, that the source of rights and obli-

[1]There seems to be no doubt that Bentham, in confounding general and individual utility, was himself deceived by the ambiguity of the term, and that he continued, during a long life, to be unconscious of his error. But what is stranger is that his followers generally, including Mr. Mill, as we have seen, seem to participate in the delusion.

34

gations, and the paramount standard of justice, are to be found in the Sovereign Will.[1]

§ 2. The theory of Bentham and Austin does not rest upon the principle of utility, but upon another principle, namely, *the definition of the law as being the command or expressed will of the sovereign or supreme power in the state.*

The theory, in other words, regards all law as **merely** *lex*, and may, therefore, with propriety, be called the *legal* theory of jurisprudence, and thus distinguished from the *jural* theory, or **theory** that regards the law in the sense of *jus.*

The definition, however, is apparently **inconsistent with** the fact that the greater part of **the law is not of statutory origin, but** consists largely of **custom,** and **has been developed** by the courts in the administration **of justice.** To meet this point, Austin is compelled **to** assert *that judicial decisions are, in effect, laws, or expressions of the will of the sovereign, through the judges as its officers; and that in the development of the law, the judges in fact perform the functions of legislators; and that custom does not in fact constitute a part of the law until it has been recognized by the courts.* Thus custom, until it **enters** into judicial **decisions, is not** law, and judicial **decisions in** their essential **nature,** do not differ from statutes; and hence all **parts of the law come** under the definition, and the whole law, is composed of statutes merely.

But, as we have observed, the principal subject with which the law has to deal is "*rights*"; and the principles by which these are determined, or, in other words, the principles observed by the courts in determining them, constitute **a part of** the law, and indeed nearly the whole of the law of private right (*jus privatum*). *Hence, if the law is wholly an expression of the will of the state, these principles come under the definition of laws; and rights, which are determined by them, are in fact determined by the will of the state, and are mere creatures of that will.*

But, under the **term** *right*, is included **every** claim that men can have to personal liberty or security, and to the acquisition and use of property, to the enjoyment of **the family** relations, and even to life itself; and *hence, if rights are mere creatures of the sovereign will, the power or right of the sovereign over the property, the liberty, and even the lives of its subjects must be absolute or unlimited.*

[1]Jur., pp. 91, 94, 109, 112, 221.

An apparently similar, but, as will be seen, in reality, an essentially different proposition, is also asserted by Austin, viz:

"It follows from the essential difference of a positive law, and from the nature of sovereignty and independent political society, *that the power of a monarch, properly so-called, or the power of a sovereign number in its collective and sovereign capacity, is incapable of legal limitation.* A monarch or sovereign number bound by **a legal** duty were subject to a higher or superior sovereign; **that** is * * * were sovereign, and not **sovereign.** *Supreme power limited by positive law is* **a flat contradiction** *in terms."*

And from this he draws another and quite a different inference, viz: *That "every free government is legally despotic";* which he says is "the same proposition dressed in different phrase." But this is not the case. For to say that the government is "legally despotic," is to say that despotic power is conferred upon it by law; which is obviously false, and, according to Austin's theory, impossible.

It follows, as a corollary from the above propositions, that the notion of natural rights *is a mere delusion, and that such rights can have no existence.* For, if natural rights do exist they must avail, *ex* **vi termini,** against all men, whether vested with political power, or mere private individuals; and the power of the sovereign would thus be limited, which is contrary to the hypothesis.

The theory also involves the denial of moral distinctions as commonly understood. For the term "rights," in its ordinary and proper sense, connotes the quality of rightness, and therefore refers to, and implies some standard of right and wrong by which the validity of rights is to **be** determined. To assert, therefore, that rights **rest** for their existence exclusively upon the will of the government is **to identify** that will with the standard referred to, and to assert that conformity or non-conformity to it, of itself constitutes right and wrong; which is in effect to deny the existence of any natural standard; for whatever the standard of right may be, it must necessarily be paramount, to and exclusive of any other.

Indeed, apart from this consideration, it is impossible **to** conceive of any ground upon **which** the principles of justice, or those principles which relate to rights, can **be denied,** and at the same time any **other moral** principles admitted;

for these, of all moral convictions, are the most clear and definite, and apparently the most certain; and it would therefore seem that they must constitute the last strong-hold of morality to be surrendered, and that, if the conception of rights, so universal and profound, is a delusion, *a fortiori* our other moral convictions must be so.

Accordingly, Hobbes, as we have seen, expressly asserts that the will of the government is the supreme standard of right; and that the terms "right" and "wrong," "just" and "unjust," signify nothing more than conformity, or non-conformity to its will; and Bentham and Austin in effect assert the same proposition. For though they hold that utility constitutes the essence of right, yet they also assert that it is too uncertain and indefinite to serve as a practical standard; and that of necessity, therefore, the government must be the sole and supreme judge of what utility may require.

The difference, therefore, is only in the manner in which they arrive at the same conclusions,—Hobbes, for that purpose, inventing the fiction of a social compact, and Bentham and Austin making use of the theory of utility; for they both in the end assert that the will of the sovereign is the supreme rule, and that the obligation of conforming to it is paramount to every other.

So paradoxical, however, is this, and the conclusion as to the non-existence of rights, that the legists generally, since the time of Bentham, have found it necessary, apparently, to recede somewhat from these extreme, but logical views upon the subject, or at least to explain and modify them in such a manner as to be less shocking to the common sense of ordinary persons.

Accordingly, Austin and the later writers of his school assert a distinction between *legal* and *moral* rights, and thereby seem to admit the existence of natural rights of a certain kind. But they are careful to explain and to insist that *such rights are not rights in a proper sense, but mere moral claims*, which the party interested is not at liberty to enforce, and which all, including the state, are at liberty to violate. *In effect, therefore, they assert equally with Bentham that there are no rights but legal rights, and that it is these alone which the courts undertake to enforce, or with which the jurist is in any way concerned.*

CHAPTER V.

§ **1.** The theory of Austin has never been received by the jurists of other countries; and, indeed, as Sir Henry Maine remarks, there seem to be " no signs of its being known on the continent at all." But in England it is now generally accepted; and, indeed, is there so firmly established as to have put a stop almost entirely to all independent investigation in jural science. The result has been, that the works of the recent English jurists, which we are about to examine, will be found in the main to consist of mere glosses or commentaries on the views of Austin; and the value of this literature must therefore depend upon two considerations, namely, the merit of Austin's work, and the greater or less success with which it has been reproduced by the writers referred to.

The writings of Austin present three characteristic features, by which the merit of his work is to be judged. These are, his theory, as to which, as this work is almost wholly devoted to its consideration, nothing further need be said here; his method; and the use he has made of the material furnished by the Roman Jurists, or rather by the modern German writers on the Roman Law.

With regard to the Roman Law, it will be sufficient to say that it furnished a favorable subject for the exercise of Austin's remarkable analytical genius; and that, in consequence, though his views are distorted by his peculiar theory, his analysis of the conceptions of the Roman jurists is of the greatest interest and utility. And it is but just to admit that, in this respect, the merits of Austin's work have been fairly reproduced by the later writers of his school. We may, therefore, pass at once to the consideration of his method.

The method of Austin can be described only by saying simply that it is strictly logical; but, without explanation, this expression will perhaps carry with it but little significance to the average reader. The method consists in the accurate statement or formulation of first principles, and in reasoning accurately from proposition to proposi-

4

tion, precisely as in geometry. Hence, such reasoning has been called, by those who would depreciate it, geometrical or mathematical ; and, though the expression is improper,—because the terms used can be applied with propriety to geometry or mathematics only,—yet the idea intended to be conveyed is correct ; for there is, in fact, no essential distinction between geometrical, or mathematical, and other kinds of deductive reasoning,—the superior certainty of the former being wholly due to the greater definiteness and accuracy of the terms used. The same method, therefore, that applies to mathematics is equally applicable, and,—though fallen into disuse,—equally essential, to the moral sciences generally ; in which the connection between the conclusions reached and the premises is equally certain as in the mathematics; so that, in fact, all true reasoning is demonstrative or apodictive. Accordingly, we find in Austin's reasoning,—and, this is its distinguishing characteristic,—the closest resemblance to that of Euclid and other geometricians. And in this he differs from the great mass of writers, ancient and modern ; for it is a fact, undoubtedly true, though but little appreciated, that men of great logical genius, like Hobbes and Austin, are as uncommon as great poets, or great generals, or great statesmen.

Hence, naturally, it has resulted that the peculiar merit of Austin in this respect has not been reproduced in the works of the later English jurists, who have altogether failed to appreciate the nature and value of his method, and while accepting generally his conclusions have not hesitated to reject such as do not suit them ; though, in fact, all the points of his theory are so bound together by the iron chain of his logic, that not one can be rejected by itself, and though the necessity of rejecting any one of them must be taken as a *reductio ad absurdum* of the whole theory.

SIR HENRY MAINE.

§ 2. Of the truth of these observations, the views of Sir Henry Maine offer a striking illustration. The historical works of this author are interesting and valuable, and they are distinguished by the extent of knowledge displayed, and by the fairness with which facts are ascertained and stated, without regard to their consistency or inconsistency with the preconceived theory of the author. His reputation as a historian is, therefore, well deserved. But it must be said of him, as was said of Puffendorf by Leibnitz, that he was *virum parum jurisconsultus et minime philosophus*. For the test of merit in scientific jurisprudence and philosophy generally is consistency, and capacity to perceive clearly the significance of the facts with which the author deals; and in this he was deficient; as may be sufficiently shown by reference to his views on two important points, selected out of many others that might be cited.

(1.) He accepts and **formally endorses** the theory of Austin; but at the same time he admits, and even takes great pains to **prove that it is** historically false, or in other words, **that it is not founded on** fact.

"**Nobody**," he says, (alluding to what he calls the "remarkable analysis of legal **conceptions effected by** Bentham and Austin,") "who has not **mastered the elementary** parts of that analysis, can hope to have clear ideas of law or jurisprudence." And this analysis, he says, "tallies **exactly** with the facts of mature jurisprudence, and with a little straining of language may be made to correspond in **form with** all law, of all kinds, at all epochs." But, he adds, there are certain errors "into which it is apt to lead us on **points of** historical jurisprudence"; for "it is curious that the further we penetrate into the primitive history of thought, the further we find ourselves from a conception of the law which at all resembles a compound of the elements which Bentham and Austin determined."

"Without the most violent forcing of language, **it is** impossible to apply these terms—*command*, **sovereign**, *obligation, sanction, right*—to the customary laws **under** which the Indian Village communities have lived for centuries, practically knowing no other law civilly obligatory." "**Nor in the sense** of the analytical jurists **is there** right or duty in an **Indian** Village community." "**And** hence, under the system of Bentham and Austin, **the** customary law of India would have to be called *morality*— an inversion of language which scarcely requires to be formally protested against."[1]

But he concludes: "Whenever you introduce any one of the legal conceptions defined by the analysis of Bentham and Austin, you introduce all the others by a **process** which is apparently inevitable. **No** better proof could be

[1] Village Communities, 66-68.

40

given that, though it be improper to employ these terms
—*sovereign, subject, command, obligation, right, sanction*
—of law in certain stages of human thought, they nevertheless correspond to a stage to which law is steadily
tending, and which it is sure ultimately to reach."[1]

The effect of which in plain language is, that Bentham's
and Austin's conception of the law has never in fact been
historically realized ; but is to be regarded merely as an
ideal towards which the law is tending, and which it is
ultimately to reach ; or, in other words, that the theory
is not a true conception of the law as it is, or as it ever
has been, but of the law as the author thinks it ought to
be, and as he thinks it is tending to become, namely,—
a mere collection of statutes.

Of this new theory, the only proof adduced by the
author is the coherency of Austin's argument, or, in other
words, the logical and therefore necessary connection between his conclusions and his assumed premise, than
which he thinks " no better proof could be given." But
obviously this conclusion is illegitimate ; for in deductive
reasoning, however conclusive be the argument, the conclusion is merely hypothetical, and its absolute truth
must depend upon the truth of the premise assumed ;
which, in this case, is that all law is in fact a mere expression of the legislative will. Hence, the conclusion
reached by Sir Henry Maine, that this is not the case, must
be taken as a complete refutation of Austin's theory. And
this, at times, he himself seems to realize. "There is,"
he says, " such wide-spread dissatisfaction with existing
theories of jurisprudence, and so general a conviction that
they do not really solve the question they pretend to dispose of, as to justify suspicion that some line of inquiry,
necessary to a perfect result, has been incompletely followed or altogether omitted by their authors."[2]

His own theory, that the statutory form is the ideal to
which the law is tending, although to some extent rendered
plausible by existing notions in England, is utterly without
verification ; and fortunately its realization is as impracticable as it would be disastrous to the welfare of mankind.

(2.) The remaining point to which we will allude is
the view taken by Maine of the law of nature, which, like
other modern English jurists, he looked upon as a " theory
plausible and comprehensive, but absolutely unverified."

[1] Id. 69, 70.
[2] Ancient Law, Chapter V.

This opinion, however, seems to have **arisen from a** mis-conception, on his part, of the origin **and meaning** of the conception of the *jus naturale* or law of nature; **of** which he says: "The Roman juristconsults borrowed **from** Greece the doctrine of **the** natural state of man and natural society, anterior to the organization of commonwealths governed by positive laws;"[1] in which doctrine he seems **to** think the origin of the conception is **to be found.** But the term *jus naturale*, as used by jurists, **or as** it should **be** translated, *natural right* or *law*, has no sort of **connection** with the hypothesis of **a state** of nature. **As used by the** Roman jurists, it is but another **name** for the *jus gentium*, which is defined by them as being the law (*jus*) "**which** natural reason has established among men," and which "**is** observed generally among all peoples"; **and is so** called "**as** being the law which all **peoples use.**" And this conception is obviously taken **from the** "*nomos koi-mos*" or "common law" of Aristotle, which **precisely corresponds with** it, and which is defined **by him** precisely **in the same way, viz: as being the law** "which is con-**formable** merely to the dictates of nature," and which is "recognized among all men." That in **Aristotle's** mind it had no reference to the admittedly **impossible hypothe-**sis of a state of nature, is sufficiently shown **by his defini-**tion of man as being **merely a** political **animal** (*zoon politi-kon*), and by his conception of natural **right or justice as** being part of the law of **a state ;** which accords precisely with the opinion of Hobbes, that "**the** law of nature is part of the civil **law of** all **commonwealths of the world.**" So also the Roman jurists regarded the *jus gentium* or *jus naturale*, not as the code originally existing **in a state of nature, but as part of** the actual law, or, as elsewhere said **by** the author himself, "**as** something belonging **to the** present, **something** entwined with the existing institu-tions."[2]

This, as we shall see, has also been uniformly the con-ception of our own jurists, prior to the time of **Austin ;** though with us the term *law of nature* is seldom used, but more generally in its place the term *reason*. For, as said by St. Germain, "it is not used among them **that be learned** in the laws of England to reason what thing is commanded or prohibited by the law of nature, and what not. But * * * when anything is grounded upon

[1] Ancient Law, 54, 68, **70, 71.**
[2] Id., 70–71.

the law of nature, they say that reason will that such a thing be done; and if it be prohibited by the law of nature, they say that it is against reason, or that reason will not suffer it to be done." (Doctor and Student, Mitchell, Clark & Co., Cincinnati, 1874.)

And this gives the precise meaning of this much-abused doctrine of the law of nature, which simply asserts that reason, justice, or right is part of the law,— a proposition almost universally asserted by jurists, and of the truth of which there cannot be any manner of doubt. And of its truth, indeed, no more striking proof can be given than in the observations of Sir Henry Maine on the part it performed in the development of the Roman law; viz, that "the progress of the Romans in legal improvement was astonishingly rapid as soon as stimulus was applied to it by the theory of natural law"; and, that "he knew of no reason why the law of the Romans should be superior to that of the Hindoos, unless the theory of natural law had given it a type of excellence different from the usual one."[1]

§ 3. Mr. Harrison's views of Austin's theory—as elaborated in several essays in the Fortnightly Review—are merely a somewhat exaggerated form of those of Sir Henry Maine, and are cited here in order to bring out more strongly the inconsistencies of that author. In his opinion, as in that of Sir Henry Maine, Austin's theory "still remains to Englishmen the foundation of rational jurisprudence"; and "in Austin, English law found the first conception of an abstract jurisprudence." But the theory, he thinks, "may be reduced to a very small number of very simple propositions; and the truth of these propositions has been asserted in much too absolute a way. For * * * they depend for their truth on assumptions which are very far from being universally true in fact, and they require qualifications which very much reduce their scientific value as social laws."

From this, it may be observed, it is obvious that the author has failed to appreciate the essential characteristics of Austin's method of reasoning; which, in fact, is the only method that can be deemed truly scientific. For, in logic, if a proposition be not altogether true, it is to be regarded as false; and it is logically absurd to say that its truth can be exaggerated, or that it can be asserted in "too absolute a way." So, if Austin's conclusions are

[1] Ancient Law, 56, 75.

not wholly true, either his reasoning is **wrong or** his premises untrue; and in either case his conclusions are wholly unwarranted, and must, therefore, be **wholly rejected,** unless some other line of reasoning can **be found to** support them.

This is attempted by Mr. Harrison, but hardly **with** success. His view is that Austin's definition of the **law** and of sovereignty, though absolutely unverified, and indeed unsusceptible of verification, **must, for some reason** not very apparent, **be accepted as a convenient** hypothesis. " The lawyer," **he says,** "has to assume law as resting on the single force of **sovereign authority ; whilst in** other branches of thought **we could** only assume this hypothesis with the certainty **of** ending in confusion and positive error. *Politically* **and** *socially* speaking, law rests on something more than **force.** *Juridically* speaking, it rests on force and force alone." **And** he adds : " As Sir Henry Maine shows, **the** theory excludes from **view** the mass of historical conditions which, **in almost every** society known to us, gives sovereignty **its social** efficacy and its distinctive character." But, " on the other hand, all this is just what the lawyer has to exclude from his view by a scientific artifice." " The result is that the Austinian conception of sovereignty is **a** perfectly sound conception when read in the light of **the** assumptions by which it is qualified and limited to the sphere to which it belongs. * * * But as **a general** proposition of human society, without **the prefixed** qualifications, **it is quite** assailable and not very intelligible. A real step was taken in the history of scientific jurisprudence when Sir Henry Maine pointed out the conditions under which the definitions of Austin must be read—conditions, I **think,** rather **ignored by** Austin himself."

In which last opinion the author is doubtless right. Austin **always had a** clear and distinct meaning, and meant what he said ; and had it occurred to him that **his** theory needed such qualifications, he would doubtless **have** abandoned it. Nor is it easy to understand how it can still **be** adhered to by Mr. Harrison and Sir Henry Maine. **For** their proposition, in plain **words, is** simply the obviously untenable one, that the theory is, **in** fact, false, but, **for some** inconceivable reason, must, " by a scientific artifice," **be** regarded by lawyers as true ; or, in other words, be made use of as a convenient legal fiction.

§ 4. Mr. Pollock criticizes Austin for devoting so much of his work to the theory of morality, and in this Mr. Harrison concurs.

"I think it a mistake," the former says, "to preface the study of legal conceptions by an exposition of transcendental ethics, and not less a mistake to preface it, as Austin did, by an exposition of the principle of utility. I do not see that a jurist is bound to be a moral philosopher more than other men." "In other words, our English school holds that the absolute law, which is or should be the origin or pattern of all existing law—*naturrecht*, as the Germans call it,—either does not exist, or does not concern lawyers more than any one else."[1] But in this Messrs. Pollock and Harrison are less logical than Hobbes, Bentham, and Austin, all of whom clearly perceived that their conception of the law, and the resulting conception of absolute sovereignty were, in fact, not only inconsistent with the notion of the existence of natural rights, or natural justice,—which is admitted by Mr. Pollock,—but also with the conception of right and wrong as commonly conceived. For, as we have observed,[2] the very conception of rights connotes, and necessarily implies, the existence of a standard of right and wrong; and hence, to assert that rights are the mere creatures of the sovereign will, is to assert that that will is the paramount standard of right and wrong. He, therefore, who asserts the definition of the law as being a mere expression of the sovereign will, logically asserts the absolute right of the sovereign over the property, the liberty, and the lives of its subjects, and denies the existence of all human rights, and, consequently, of all moral distinctions. To Hobbes, Bentham and Austin,—as it must be to all logical minds,—it was impossible to retain their confidence in the premises assumed without asserting these conclusions. And, especially with reference to natural justice, was this necessity apparent to them. For, to quote Bentham, "there is no reasoning" in any other way "with fanatics armed with natural rights." For, as they clearly perceived, there is no way of separating morality from law otherwise than by abolishing it, and to assert the existence of morality in any other than the peculiar form in which it is asserted by them is to abandon what was regarded

[1]Essays in Jurisprudence and Ethics.
[2]Ante, p. 35.

by them as an essential and fundamental part of their theory.[1]

§ 5. Mr. Markby is one of the most pronounced adherents of Austin's theory, which he regards as " pretty well established," and as " generally accepted by English jurists." But he agrees with Mr. Harrison and Sir Henry Maine, in asserting that the theory is not historically verified ; and also with the former and Mr. Pollock, in asserting that the theory does not rest "upon any theory of religion or morality," but "might be accepted by a Hindoo, by a Mohammedan, or by a Christian,"—propositions which, as we have seen, in effect amount to a repudiation of Austin's theory.

But perhaps the most radical departure from Austin's views is the proposition, asserted by Mr. Markby, that there are principles or rules of decision habitually used by the courts which are no part of the law, and which do not become such by reason of the decision. And in this, as we shall see, Mr. Holland in effect agrees.

" There are cases," says Mr. Markby, " in which rules are adopted and acted on by judges which have not hitherto existed as law, and which judges do not even pretend to make law by acting upon them. In other words, I think judges constantly arrive at a point at which they refer to a standard which is not a legal one. This takes place frequently in modern English law." And he adds : "The very notion that a rule can by any possibility be transformed into law by judicial recognition is quite a modern one, even in England ; and nothing of the kind has ever been recognized except in England, and in countries that have formed their legal systems under the influence of England. * * * And yet we find that everywhere judges unhesitatingly refer to the principles of jurisprudence as generally recognized, to the principles of equity, and to the guidance of common sense, and they take their guidance as willingly from these sources as from any other."

" This admission seems to place the disciples of Austin

---

[1] "The first ray of light," says Dumont, "which struck the mind of Bentham in the study of the law, was the perception that *natural right,* the *original pact,* the *moral sense,* the *notion of just and unjust,* which are *used* to explain everything, were at bottom nothing but those innate *ideas* of which Locke has so clearly shown the falsity." Introd. to the Principles of the Civil Code. And in the same way, as we have seen, the terms *conscience, moral sense,* and similar terms, were regarded by Austin as mere cloaks for hypocrisy and sinister interest. (Infra, p. 62.)

46

in a difficulty. It seems to show that Austin's conception of law is not adequate, even as applied to modern English law; and that it is equally inadequate, if we look into our own past history, or into the condition of law in other countries. In short, it seems to show that Austin's conception of law fails as a general or scientific conception."[1]

And so it does, though the author attempts unsuccessfully to reconcile the contradiction. For the essential characteristic of Austin's theory is not merely to restrict the term, law, to statutory enactments, legislative or judicial, but also to extend its application so as to include all rules and principles of judicial decision; and to hold that decisions may be made, or, in other words, that rights may be determined, by principles not forming part of the law, such as those of jurisprudence, or natural justice, or equity, is to surrender his whole position.

§ 6. Mr. Holland accepts all the conclusions of Austin. "The sovereign part of the State," he says, "is omnipotent"; "an act is, strictly speaking, never unconstitutional unless it is also illegal, and can never be either if it is the act of the sovereign power." Rights are created by the sovereign will; "the immediate objects of law are the creation and protection of legal rights"; "that which gives validity to a legal right is in every case the force which is lent to it by the State"; "international law can be described as law only by courtesy." And the same is true of constitutional law.

Nevertheless, he abandons the definition of Austin, that the law is merely an expression of the will of the State,—which is the premise from which all his conclusions are deduced,—and adopts an essentially different definition; which is, that "a law is a general rule of external conduct enforced by a sovereign power," and the law "an aggregate of laws." To this definition there is no objection, except that it is not, in a true sense, a definition at all; in which respect it differs from that of Austin, which is a true or essential definition. From the latter, all the conclusions of Austin's theory may be logically deduced; but they cannot be deduced from Holland's definition. Nor, indeed, can anything be inferred from it; for it is equally consistent with Austin's theory, and also with that which asserts that justice, or natural right, or,—to state it in the form most obnoxious to the modern English jurist,—the law of nature is, as Hobbes asserts,

[1]Elementary Law, §§23-4.

a part of the law; and with this Austin's definition is altogether inconsistent.

Hence, in abandoning Austin's definition, Holland loses the sole foundation upon which Austin's, and his own conclusions rest; and in his system they remain mere gratuitious assumptions, without even an attempted argument to support them.

Mr. Holland also dissents from Mr. Austin's proposition that custom does not become law until it is recognized by the courts.

"The state," he says, "through its delegates, the judges, undoubtedly grants recognition as law to such customs as come up to a certain standard of general reception and usefulness. To these the Courts give operation, not merely prospectively from the date of such recognition, but also retrospectively; so far implying that the custom was law before it received the stamp of judicial authentication. The contrary view supported by Austin is at variance with fact. * * * Not having a code ready at their hand, with rules for every emergency, they [the judges] have invoked, as the *ratio* of their decisions, not only equity, or the generally acknowledged view of what is fair, and previous decisions of the Court, upon the faith of which it is to be presumed that people have been acting, but also customs established among and by the people at large, as presumably embodying the rules which the people have found suitable to the circumstances of their lives. The Courts have, therefore, long ago established as a fundamental principle of law, subject, of course, in each case to many restrictions and qualifications, that, in the absence of a specific rule of written law, regard is to be had, in looking for the rule which governs a given set of circumstances, not only to equity and to previous decisions, but also to custom."[1]

This, in effect, is to assert with Hobbes and jurists generally, that natural right—of which equity is but another name—as also custom, is part of the law; but it is inconsistent with Austin's theory, and amounts to a repudiation of it.

§ 7. Mr. Amos is also a pronounced admirer of Austin. To him was due, he says, " the deliverance of the law from the dead body of morality "; and he " may be said to have been the true founder of the Science of Law, if indeed such honor could ever belong to any one man ";[2] or, in other words, to him " the conscious establishment of the legal science must properly be attributed."[1] He also unequivocally accepts the definition of Austin : " A law," he says, " is a command of the Supreme Political Authority of a state,"[2] and the law is a body of such commands."[3]

But it follows from this definition, and Austin emphatically asserts, that neither International nor Constitutional Law is law in the proper sense, but each is nothing more than positive morality. It would seem, therefore, that Mr. Amos, in accepting his definition, committed himself to this proposition. But such is not the case.

" The true lesson," he says, " enforced by the seemingly impracticable phenomenon presented by the body of rules forming the bulk of what is known as the Law of Nations, * * * is, that the distinguishing characteristics of true law must be sought for somewhere else than in the nature of the authority from which it proceeds, and in the certainty of the punishment by which its infraction is intended ; "[4] and accordingly he propounds the question: " Whether the definition of the term law, as given by the most recent and celebrated school of English legal writers, is not based on too restricted a conception of the phenomena to which it relates ? "[5]

On the same grounds, he is also of the opinion with reference to Constitutional Law, that, though " as a matter of ethical or historical research, the use of the word ' morality ' is, neither inappropriate nor uninteresting," yet, " just as in the parallel case of International Law, the rules in question are as unlike as possible to moral principles and maxims, and are as like as possible to genuine laws."[6]

There could not be a more perfect demonstration of the falsity of Austin's definition, or a more conclusive refutation of the theory based upon it, than this ; but apparently a *reductio ad absurdum* is not regarded by Mr. Amos as a legitimate mode of argument.

§ 8.   One other case will be referred to as illustrating our thesis. The doctrine of absolute sovereignty is established, or rather the attempt is made to establish it, by Hobbes and Bentham and Austin, by extended and elaborate reasoning. But lately a shorter method has been discovered, which I find attributed to Professor Huxley, in a collection of essays lately published, under the attractive but misleading title of " *A Plea for Liberty*,"

[1]Id. 8. [3]Id. 1. [5]Id. 322.
[2]Jurisprudence, 73. [4]Science of Law, 324. [6]Id. 115.

and which, I may say in passing, is calculated to remind one of old Joab's treatment of his comrade, Amaza, when he took him by the beard to kiss him, saying : "Art thou in health, my brother?" and stabbed him under the fifth rib.

It is as follows :

"The power of a State may be defined as the resultant of all the social forces acting within a definite area. 'It follows,' says Professor Huxley, with characteristic thoroughness of logic, ' that no limit is or can be set to State interference.'"

From this the author proceeds to argue, with Hobbes and Austin, that "the power of the State is absolute"; that "it still remains unlimited despotism, as Hobbes assumes"; "that rights, when created, are created by the strong for its own good pleasure"; and so on, to all their conclusions.[1]

But, obviously, the argument consists of a mere rhetorical artifice, and can hardly be accepted as a satisfactory substitute for the stalwart logic of Hobbes and Austin. The term *forces*, in its primary sense, denotes merely physical forces. These operate under fixed laws, from which, if the direction and intensity of any number of forces operating on any point are known, the resultant can be mathematically determined. But nothing of this applies to human powers, or to social or moral forces. As to these, the expressions *forces, and resultant of forces*, are purely metaphorical. In a direct sense the proposition, if it has any meaning at all, amounts only to the platitude that the actual power of the government is, in fact, the preponderating power in the State. It says nothing with reference to the rightful power, or right of the State, which is the only material point. Hence its fallacy consists in the neglect to observe the ambiguity of the term power, to which I have already alluded, (*supra, p.* 24) and in thus confounding *mere* power, or might, with *rightful power*, or right. In the premises, the term is used in the former senses ; in the conclusion, in the latter ; and thus the argument, with all its supposed "thoroughness of logic," presents a transparent case of that most common and most destructive of all fallacies, an ambiguous middle.

[1]Strangely enough the preface to this work is contributed by Mr. Herbert Spencer, who is thus apparently made to stand sponsor for a doctrine, doubtless as abhorrent to his soul as it was to that of Aristotle; in whose view, "to intrust man with supreme power was to give it to a wild beast."

CHAPTER VI.

§ 1. The theory of Austin, as we have observed, rests wholly upon his definition of the law, as a first principle. This was taken by him from Bentham, who in turn took it from Blackstone, — who as a lawyer ought to have known better; and neither of them seem ever to have suspected that any doubt could be entertained of its truth. But in fact,—as perhaps sufficiently appears from what has been said, and as will be more fully shown in the sequel,— it is an essentially false description of the law and owes its plausibility solely to the verbal identity of the terms, " *a law*,".and " the law "; of the former of which only is it a correct definition. For the term, " *a law*," in our language commonly denotes merely a statute or act of legislation; but the term " *the* law " denotes that aggregate of rules and principles by which in every State the mutual rights and obligations of its citizens are regulated, and the decisions of its Courts, in matters of private right, determined ; and which in other languages than our own is termed *Jus, Droit, Recht,* or by some other term equivalent to our word *Right*.

To infer from this usage that the law consists merely of right or justice would,—as Austin and his school have not failed to insist,—be unphilosophic ; but it is equally illegitimate to assume,—as they do,—from the different usage of our own language, that the law consists entirely of statutes or laws ; for obviously the question is one that can be determined only by an analysis and examination of the law as it actually exists.

To this test the question must ultimately be submitted ; but it usually, and perhaps universally happens that a false theory carries in itself, in the inconsistencies or absurdities logically involved in it, the seeds of its own destruction ; and thus generally, to logical minds, the readiest means of refuting it is to develop its logical consequences.

This, in the case of Austin,— as may be seen by reference to the statement of his theory heretofore given,[1]— has, in the main, been effected with wonderful logical in-

[1] *Ante*, p. 34 e *seq.*

trepidity, by the author himself; but there are certain points with regard to which he seems to have failed to perceive the consequences involved in his views. These relate (1) to the doctrine of sovereignty, (2) to the nature of judicial decisions, and (3) to the nature of rights, and will be considered in the order stated. Afterwards (4) it will be shown that, by an apparently slight modification of Austin's theory, already suggested by Markby and Holland, it can be reconciled with truth and reason, and all objection to it, except perhaps on the score of impropriety of language, removed.

§ 2. (1) Two arguments are used by Austin to establish the absolute right or power of the sovereign, or supreme government, viz: the argument from utility, and the argument from the definition of the law. The former has already been touched upon in our review of Hobbes, and it will be sufficient to repeat here that while it clearly establishes the necessity of government, and also that it should be vested with all the powers or rights necessary and proper to the efficient performance of its functions,—which must necessarily be great,—it does not establish, or tend to establish, that these should be absolute or unlimited. On the contrary, with reference to the rightful power, or right of the government, it seems to establish the proposition of Rutherford, that the " civil power is in its own nature a limited power : as it arose at first from the social union, so it is limited by the ends and purposes of such union, whether it be exercised, as it is in democracies, by the body of the people ; or, as it is in monarchies, by one single person.[2] And with reference to its

[2] Institutes of Natural Law. p. 393.

actual power, the most obvious dictate of utility is that it should, as far as practicable, be limited to such power as may be necessary for the performance of its functions.

Hence, it is obvious, the doctrine of absolute sovereignty—if it can be maintained—must rest upon the other argument urged by Austin, namely, the argument from the definition of the law, of which it must be regarded as a mere corollary.

This definition, as I have said, is obviously untenable ; but for the present, as it is proposed to examine merely the consistency of Austin's famous argument,—which not only convinced himself, but has carried conviction to the minds of two generations of English jurists, and is still triumphantly regarded by them as the rock upon which their faith is founded,—the definition will be assumed to be true.

The argument is in effect that it follows (*ex vi termini*) from the definition of the law, as consisting of the commands of the sovereign, that the power of the sovereign cannot be limited by law, or, in the language of Austin, " is incapable of legal limitation.[1]"

In this proposition, it will be observed, Austin uses the term, sovereign, as denoting merely the " *supreme government*," or supreme political organization of a state, (in his own language " the monarch," or " the sovereign number in its collegiate and sovereign capacity ") ; and, consequently, the law is to be regarded as consisting of the commands of this sovereign, *i. e.*, of the supreme government, whether consisting of a monarch or a sovereign body.

Thus construing the terms, the argument is obviously conclusive, for it simply asserts that the power of the sovereign or supreme government cannot be limited by its own commands,—a proposition universally true, not only of sovereigns, but of all persons,—real or fictitious,—whatever. But the proposition,—which, thus construed, is entirely innocent, and, indeed, without significance,—is habitually used by Austin and his school, as though equivalent to the proposition that the power of the government is unsusceptible of being limited by statutory enactments,—a proposition essentially different, and, at least to an American, obviously false; for in this country the powers both of the Federal and of the State governments are, in fact, limited by organic statutory laws, imposed by Constitutional conventions, or constituent assemblies ; and it cannot be doubted, either that our governments are supreme governments, or that our constitutional enactments are statutes or laws in the strictest sense.

This difficulty is, indeed, considered by Austin, and solved to the entire satisfaction of himself and his followers ; but a very brief examination of his argument will be sufficient to show that it is untenable, and that it in fact presents a transparent case of *ignoratio elenchi ;* of which the most common, and dangerous form is,—as is here illustrated,—to use a conclusion, true only in a particular sense of the terms in which it is stated, as though applicable to other cases where the terms are used in a different sense.

Here, the ambiguity is in the term, sovereign; which is

[1] Suprr p, 35.

commonly used to denote, not only the supreme government, or political organization of the state, but also the state, or the people, as distinguished from the government. These two senses of the term are obviously confounded in the argument of Austin. For, bearing in mind this double sense of the term, there is nothing contradictory in saying that the supreme government may be at once "sovereign" and "not sovereign"; *i. e.*, "sovereign," as being the supreme government, but "not sovereign," as being the state; or, in saying that the government, though sovereign, is subject to a higher sovereign: namely, the state; or, in saying that its powers may be limited, as in this country, by statutory laws imposed by constitutional conventions. Nor is it an answer to this proposition to say,—as is undoubtedly true,—that a constitutional convention is itself a legislative assembly, or, as Austin expresses it, " an extraordinary and ulterior legislature," (Jur. 254); for it is not true that such a convention is a government, even when in session; still less after it has been dissolved, and its members mingled with the body of the people.

It is, however, a cardinal point in the theory of Austin that a *sanction*, or liability to punishment, is an essential element in a law; and hence it is argued that, as constitutional laws have no power behind them to inflict punishment for their violation other than the government itself, they are not in fact laws, except so far as the government may choose to adopt them. But, admitting for the sake of the argument, that the premises are correct, the conclusion, it can be readily shown, does not follow.

Here, also, the fallacy lies in a misuse of the terms sovereign and sovereignty, which will, therefore, require further explanation. These terms, as we have seen, were originally applied to the case of a single sovereign or monarch; and in this sense,—which is their only proper sense,—their meaning is clear and distinct; a sovereign is a monarch, in whom is vested the *highest*, or supreme power in the state; and sovereignty is the power vested in him. But the application of the term, as we have seen, was extended by Hobbes to aristocracies, or sovereign bodies; and, since his time, has been further extended so as to embrace such composite governments as those of England and the United States; and recently it has even been used to denote mere abstractions that are not governments, as when, for instance, we speak of " the sovereignty of the people," or " of the state," as distinguished from the government, or of " the sovereignty of the law," or " of justice," or of " the sovereignty of public opinion "; all of which, even those applied to governments, are improper or figurative senses of the terms. For when the supreme government consists of more than one, whether it be a simple assembly, or a more complex organization, it is obviously what is called a corporation or body corporate; which is a fictitious or imaginary being different and distinct from the individuals of which it is constituted. This conception is, indeed, a useful one in the law, where the subject of corporations constitutes a leading topic ; and the analogy between such fictitious persons and real persons is so close, that nearly every proposition that may be predicated of the one will be true also of the other. But it is, nevertheless, unless carefully used, a very dangerous one ; for there is obviously a point beyond which the analogy breaks down, and to carry it further would be a source of error.[1]

And of this, the notion of the indivisibility of sovereign power,—which is founded wholly on the conception of government as a corporation, or fictitious being,—is a conspicuous instance. For while it is obvious that the power of a sovereign, in the proper sense, or a monarch, cannot be divided, it is equally obvious that, in the case of all other kinds of sovereigns, including simple sovereign assemblies, sovereign power is not only divisible, but is in fact necessarily divided. For the power of which we are treating is human power, or power vested in some actual human being ; and hence a sovereign power is to be defined simply as the power of an officer or department which has no superior, or which is not subordinate to any other ; and there must, therefore, be as many sovereign powers,

[1] The celebrated case of Dartmouth College vs. Woodward, (4 Wheat. 518,) furnishes a striking instance of pushing this analogy too far. In that case the principle was asserted that a charter to a corporation is a contract, which, under the constitutional provision forbidding the enactment of laws impairing the obligation of contracts, could not be altered by the State ; and the principle was held to apply to the charter of the plaintiff,—an eleemosynary corporation. But it is clear that, strictly speaking, a corporation,—which is a purely fictitious or imaginary being,—cannot itself have any rights, and that what we call the rights of a corporation are, in fact, the rights of its stockholders, creditors, or other individuals beneficially interested ; and hence that the constitutional provision can have no application, if there are no such persons,—as was in fact the case before the Court. Hence in that case, —as in all others where property has no other owner, the beneficial interest in the property of the corporation was in the State, and it could deal with it as it pleased. Or, to state the proposition more generally, all property held for charitable purposes,—at least, after the death of the donors,—belongs to the State, and may be disposed of by it according to its own views of what is right and proper.

—or, we may say, sovereigns,—as there are co-ordinate
officers or departments in the government. Thus, in the
American governments sovereign power is vested in the
President or Governor; also in Congress or the Legislature, and also in the judicial department; and these
powers are not only separate, but essentially different in
their natures, and independent of, and co-ordinate with
each other. Each department is therefore supreme or
sovereign in the province allotted to it; and there is no
reason, except for convenience, why these different, separate, independent, supreme powers should be regarded
as one. We may, indeed, if we desire, thus conceive of
the government as a fictitious or artificial person, exercis-
ing these various functions through its several departments; but back of this conception lies the fact that this
artificial person can exercise no functions whatever, except
alternately through one or the other of the supreme political organizations, or, as they may be called, sovereigns,
of which it is constituted. Hence, if we would avoid
error, when we use the terms sovereign and sovereignty,
in any other than their proper sense, as applying to a
monarch, or single sovereign. it is always to be remembered that we are dealing with a purely fictitious notion,
the creation of our own minds, which has no counterpart
in nature; or, in other words, that we are dealing with
the power, not of actual men,—with which alone jurisprudence is ultimately concerned,—but with that of a fictitious or ideal being, without intelligence, conscience, or
will. For otherwise, according to the peculiar mode in
which we may choose to construct our artificial sovereign,
—and, with reference to every complex government, our
ability to vary his nature is unlimited,—any number of
the most contradictory conclusions may be reached,—as,
for instance, in the case of our government alone, that
the sovereign power is vested in the states, regarded as an
assembly of fictitious persons or bodies politic, (which is
Austin's notion); or in the states individually; or in the
federal government, to the exclusion of the states; or in
the people of the United States collectively; or—as held
by a late writer on the constitution—in that class or number of people, or party, whose power at any time may
happen to preponderate. In short, with the power of
creating our premises at will which the use of fiction gives
us, any conclusion desired may be established.

Of this, the argument of Austin, which we are examining—viz: that ordinances or statutes enacted by constitutional conventions are not laws, for lack of sanctions to enforce them,—is an instance. For independently of the fact that the observance of such laws is enforced by fear of revolution or rebellion, or of a constitutional change of the government,—which is a sanction essentially identical in nature with the sanctions by which individuals are impelled to obedience,—the proposition is otherwise obviously false. For, while we cannot punish the fictitious being which, in corporate governments, is conceived to constitute the sovereign,—and which, in the language of an eminent jurist, has neither a soul to be saved, nor a body to be kicked—we can punish the actual human beings in whom the power is in fact vested; that is to say, the President or Governor, (or in England the ministers of the Crown,) the members of the Legislature, and the judges; and it is very certain that, if these can be restrained by the fear of punishment, we need have no fear of our imaginary Leviathan.

Indeed, as we have seen, independently of this consideration, it is obvious that, except in the case of a monarchy, absolute political power is impossible. For from the nature of the case, as was very clearly perceived by Hobbes, to divide the sovereign or supreme political power between several individuals or departments is, of necessity, to diminish or limit it; for, in such case, the power of each officer or department is limited by that of the others; and, as each part is limited, it follows that the whole must also be limited. Hence, as I have said elsewhere, the maxim "*Divide et impera*" is as obvious a principle of political organization as it is of war or diplomacy; and, indeed, it is to the application of this principle that all improvement in political organization is due.

§ 3. (2) Upon the most cursory examination of the law, with a view of testing the accuracy of Austin's definition, we are confronted with the fact already alluded to, that it consists in the main of rules and principles established by precedent or judicial decision, and that laws in the ordinary sense, or statutes, constitute but a small and comparatively unimportant part of it; which would seem to be a conclusive refutation of the definition. But, as we have seen, Austin, to meet this point, asserts that the judges, in effect, exercise legislative functions, and that their decisions are, in their essential nature, statutes or commands of the sovereign made or enacted by the judges as its sub-

ordinate officers. It is clear, therefore, that here lies a
crucial test by which the truth or falsity of the definition
is to be determined, and that, if this proposition be found
untenable, the definition must be rejected.[1]

A full discussion of this proposition would involve an
examination of the nature of the judicial function, and of
the doctrine of *stare decisis*, or of the authority of judicial
decisions,—a subject of great interest, but which would
demand a greater space than we can here give it. But, as
fortunately the subject will be more or less familiar to the
reader, it will perhaps be sufficient on these points to observe
that the proposition is opposed to the uniform opinion of
the jurists, both of our own and of the Roman law, as embodied in the maxim, *judicis est jus dicere, non dare ;* that
it is in conflict with the rule of *stare decisis*, as uniformly
interpreted by the authorities of either law ; and that it is
subversive of the supposed distinction between the several
functions of government, namely, the executive, the legislative, and the judicial, which has long since come to be
received in political science as fundamental.

But such a discussion though interesting, is, I think,
unnecessary here,—as the doctrine carries in itself its own
refutation, and can be readily disposed of,—as we have
seen is the case with other points of the theory,—by
merely considering the consequences logically involved
in it. Of these the most obvious are the following:

The doctrine in question is founded on the rule of
stare decisis,—of which indeed it purports to be but an
expression. It will therefore apply to the decisions of
the Courts on the construction and effect of statutes,
equally as to their decisions on other questions. Whatever doubts and conflicts may have arisen with reference
to the application of the rule in other respects, it has
never been suggested that there is any distinction to be
made between its application to acts of the legislature, or
ordinary statutes, and its application to rules otherwise
established. Hence it follows that the ordinary legislature cannot enact a valid law as to matters of private
right ; for such law or supposed law cannot be enforced
otherwise than by the Courts, and is, therefore, without
a sanction,—which according to the theory is an essen-

---

[1] It is worthy of remark that on this point Austin differs from Bentham, who regarded this exercise of power by the judges as a usurpa-
tion. But Austin, with a clearer perception of the logical exigencies of
the case, was compelled to invent the monstrous doctrine that the
judges are, in fact, vested with legislative power.

tial element of a true law,—until it is so recognized; and, if the Courts fail to recognize it, or give it an erroneous construction, it can never become a law. In this respect, statutes stand in precisely the same category as customs or principles of natural right; which, according to the theory, cannot become law until adopted by the Courts.

Nor can it be consistently said by Austin and his followers that the judges *ought* to carry out the enactments of the legislature. For, according to their theory, *obligation* consists merely in the liability to, and fear of, punishment; and to say that a man *ought* to do or not to do anything, or is *under obligation* to do, or not to do it, means simply that the performance or non-performance of the act is imposed upon him by the fear of impending punishment; of which in this country, and generally in others,—except in a few extreme cases, which will not materially affect the question,—the judges have no cause to have apprehension; but rather it may be said that there is no other situation in life in which stupidity and even conscious injustice can be exercised with such entire impunity as on the bench.

Nor can there be any law of any kind binding on the judges. For, being vested with legislative power, they can, if they please, disregard the decisions of their predecessors, not only with impunity, but without blame. For the legislative power is, in its essential nature, an arbitrary power, and to be exercised according to the maxim *voluntas stet pro ratione,* and the rule applies, *leges posteriores abrogant priores.*

Nor is it any answer to this to say that the judges *ought* to follow the decisions of their predecessors. Most people indeed, think that they *ought* in general to do so, and they think also that customs, when rational, and also principles of justice and right, should be observed by the Courts; but, according to the theory, these are mere *moral* considerations with which the law is not concerned.

Hence, as the ultimate consequence of the doctrine, we must conclude that law is in fact impossible, and that the sole standard of men's rights must always consist in the fluctuating and unforeseeable opinions, or rather decisions, of the Courts; and this in fact, it is to be apprehended, is something like the condition to which the influence of this pernicious doctrine upon modern lawyers has reduced the law at the present day.

§ 4. (3) It is a proposition so often stated as to have become commonplace, and that has in effect been asserted in all the fundamental laws of **our** race, from Magna Charta to the last state constitution, that it is the function **of** government to establish justice, or, in other words, to secure the observance of private rights. Verbally this proposition is admitted by the Austin school of jurists; but in effect it is denied; for, according to their definition, a right is nothing **more** than **the capacity or power** conferred upon one by **the state to control the actions of** another, or of others.[1]

In his view and **that of** his followers, therefore, the sole essential **element** in a right is power over others, conferred by **the state.** Where this exists, whether such power be right **or** wrong, just or unjust, it constitutes a right; and without it no right **can** exist. **In other** words, in their view, the terms " *a right* " or " *rights* " and the adjective " *right* " have no community **or identity** of meaning, but are merely homonymous.

Sometimes indeed, as we have observed, Austin, **and** also other legists, speak **of** *moral*, as opposed to *legal* rights,—but we are plainly told **that** this is merely for the sake of conformity to common language. " Strictly speaking," he says, " there are no rights but **those** which are creatures of the law."[2] And Bentham **is even more** emphatic. " The **word, rights,"** he says, **" the same as** the word law, **has two senses ; the one a** proper sense, the other a metaphorical **sense.** Rights, properly **so** called, are creatures of law, properly so called : real laws give birth to real rights. * * * Natural **rights are** the creatures of natural laws : they are **a metaphor which derive** their existence from another metaphor." **But obviously this** is to leave out an essential **element in the** signification of the term **"a right,"** or **"rights,"** which in its proper, **and universally received, as well as in its** etymological sense, **connotes** or **implies, as part of its** essential meaning, **the quality of rightness or rectitude;**

---

[1] " A person has a right, when the law authorizes him to exact from another an act or forbearance * * * The capacity **or** power of exacting from another acts or forbearances is nearest to a true definition." Austin, Jur. 410. To the same effect is Amos, Jur. **79.** Holland's definition is somewhat different, but, so far as bears upon the subject **of** discussion, in effect the same. According to it, a right is " a capacity residing on one man of controlling, with the assent and assistance of the state, the actions of another. That which gives validity **to a legal** right is in every case the force which is lent **to** it by the state." Jur. 8, 62.

[2] Jur. 354.

or, in other words, a right is not merely a power, but it is, *ex vi termini*, always a rightful power. Hence the so-called rights of Austin are not true rights, but merely what are called in the law actions; which are defined by the jurists, both of our own, and the Roman law, substantially in the same way.[1]

Hence, an obvious question presents itself. If it be assumed, as it is in effect assumed by this theory, that the notions of right and wrong, and of the just and unjust, as popularly conceived, are erroneous, why keep alive these delusions by transferring the use of the term "right" to another subject, to which, in its proper sense, it cannot apply, and which already has its appropriate term to denote it? Why not say at once that the law is concerned with *actions* only, and that it has nothing to do with rights of any kind? In this way the legists would rid the subject of all confusion, and would no longer delude people—and perhaps themselves—into the supposition that they are treating of rights, when they are not only treating of something essentially different, but actually denying their very existence; and the only conceivable reason why this course should not be pursued is that this sacred name, *rights*, and its correlatives, justice or right, serve as a convenient cloak which cannot be dispensed with without exposing the hideous deformity of their theory.

§ 5. (4) The above observations suggest a mode in which, by an apparently slight modification of the *legal* theory, it may be stripped of its objectionable features, and made conformable to truth and decency.

The definition of a law as an expression of the will of the state, if confined to the subject to which it relates, is unobjectionable; nor is there any objection—except that it is opposed to the more common usage—to denoting the aggregate of laws by the term, the law; nor is there any serious objection, beyond that of impropriety of language, to adopting the fiction of Hobbes, that whatever the sovereign permits he commands, and to thus extending the application of the term law so as to include not only laws

---

[1] "*Actio nihil aliud est quam jus persequendi in judicio quod alicui debitur*"; which,—as the term, *jus*, is used, in the Latin, to denote mere legal powers as well as rights,—may be translated: "An action is nothing else than the legal power of prosecuting before the Courts what is due to any one" Hence, acording to Heineccius, "An action is not a right, but a means of prosecuting a right." "*Actio non est jus, sed medium jus persequendi.*"

in the strict sense,—or statutes,—but also all arbitrary or peculiar rules and principles of the law; or in other words, so as to include the whole of the *jus civile* or *nomos idios* as conceived by the Roman lawyers, and before them by Aristotle. But in doing this we must guard against the error of supposing that the term, law, as thus defined, will include all that is now included under the term, *the law*, in its wider and more common sense of *jus*. For in this sense the law includes not only the *jus civile*, or peculiar law of the state, but also the *jus gentium*, "or *jus naturale*"; which by our new definition is excluded. Nor is it necessary for us to deny the existence of the *jus naturale*, or *natural right :* all that it is necessary to affirm is, that it is not part of the law as we now define it.

But, in accepting this view of the case, we necessarily affirm with Markby and Holland, that the judges in determining controversies will not be confined to the law, but must resort also to matters outside of the law. For it is the admitted function of the state through its judges to administer justice ; or in other words, to enforce rights; and to do this it is necessary to have resort to equity, justice, or natural right ; which terms denote merely the aggregate of the principles by which rights are determined. In other words, according to our definition, the law of private right would consist merely of the doctrine of actions; but these, according to a fundamental maxim both of our own and the Roman law, (*ubi jus ibi remedium,*) would have to be determined by a resort to the doctrine of rights, or natural right ; which, though outside of the law, would still furnish the principles by which the question of right, or in other words, the merits or justice of the case, would have to be determined. Thus modified, the theory would conform precisely to that of Hobbes ; and in this manner justice and the law instead of being antagonized, as they are under the present form of the theory, would be reconciled; and the aggregate of the two— which, as under our present hypothesis it can no longer be called *law*, we may call *jus*—will conform precisely to that which is now denoted by the term, *the law*. Hence, it will be perceived, the modification of the *legal* theory suggested by Markby and Holland, which was regarded by them as not materially affecting it, in fact essentially changes it, and in effect converts it into the *jural* theory, and themselves unconsciously from *legists* into *jurists*.

CHAPTER VII.

UTILARIANISM.[1]

§ 1. The sole function performed by the principle of utility in Austin's theory is, to establish the supremacy of government, and its further discussion might therefore be dispensed with, were it not for the fact that practically the theory is used by Bentham and Austin, and by the utilitarians generally, apparently for the purpose of destroying the moral convictions or conscience of mankind; or, in other words, for the very purpose that, Austin says, is not within its scope or object, namely, "to crush the moral sentiments" as actually existing in the general conscience.[2]

Of this, Austin's own use of the theory furnishes a type. In his view, "the *moral sense, practical principles, conscience,* * * * are merely convenient cloaks for ignorance or sinister interest;[3] and the terms *just* and *unjust*, when used otherwise than as denoting conformity, or non-conformity to the Sovereign Will, are to be regarded as "a mischievous and detestable abuse of articulate language."[4] But in his Austin was not only in error; but inconsistent; for elsewhere, in expounding the theory of utility, he is emphatic in asserting that, according to it, conduct is to be determined by rules; that such rules, from the nature of the case, must, by the great mass of mankind, be accepted "on authority, testimony, or trust"; and that the acts enjoined or forbidden by these rules are invariably accompanied by a moral sentiment or feeling, or "a sentiment or feeling of approbation or disapprobation," which is "inseparably connected in the mind with the thought or conception of such acts."[5] But when he attacks the authority of the common notions of right and wrong, justice and injustice, he forgets the true principle of his theory, and uses it as though it were an effective argument for his purpose, instead of being, as it is, an argument by which the common moral notions

---

[1] The subject of this chapter is treated in Right and Law, cited *supra*, and what is there said is here to some extent repeated ; but it is now more fully developed.

[2] Jur. 120.   [4] Id. 223.

[3] Id. 221.   [5] Jur., 118, 119, 127.

of mankind, and especially those of justice, may be vindicated. It becomes necessary, therefore, to examine the theory of utility, with a view of seeing how far its claims to supplant all others are justified ; and upon such investigation it will be found that the theory is not merely untrue, but that it is without definite signification, or, in other words, nonsensical.

It is generally assumed when we speak of the principle of utility, or, as it has come to be called, *utilitarianism*, that we have in view a single, consistent theory of morality ; but in fact there are embraced under the one name several distinct and irreconcilable theories. These grow respectively out of the several different meanings of the term, *utility ;* which, though apparently simple in meaning, is extremely ambiguous. For, it is obvious, the term is a relative one, implying some man or men whose welfare is promoted, and its meaning must therefore vary according to its correlative.

When applied to a single individual, the meaning of the term is clear. It denotes the interest or welfare of the individual referred to. When used with reference to a class, it is equally clear, properly speaking, that it denotes the interest or welfare of every individual of the class. For to say that anything is useful to two or more, or any number of men, is to say that it is useful to each of them. If this be not the case, the expression is inaccurate ; and we should say, not that it is useful to the class, but that it is useful to some, or most of the individuals composing it. Hence, to say that anything will be useful to the community, or to mankind, is to say, if we speak accurately, that it will be universally useful, — that is, useful to every individual of the community or race.

These are the only definite meanings of which the term is susceptible, and hence there can be only two admissible expressions of the principle of utility, — which may be called respectively the theory of individual, and that of universal utility ; the first of which asserts that to every individual his own good or interest is the only test of right and wrong ; and the latter, that whatever is shown to be for the good or welfare of every individual of the community or race must be right ; or, in a negative form, that whatever is pernicious or contrary to the welfare of any individual cannot be right.

This, however, is not the theory of general utility advocated by Bentham and Austin ; which is something altogether different. Properly speaking, indeed, the term *general utility* would seem to denote that which is universally useful ; but according to a common usage, and therefore allowable in familiar speech, it is also used to denote only that which is useful in most cases. But in this sense the term is not logically serviceable, for its meaning is indefinite, and unsusceptible of precise definition, and it cannot be determined what is the proportion of individuals whose welfare is to be considered,—whether a mere majority, or three-fourths, or nine-tenths, or more or less. The theory is, therefore, as we have observed, nonsensical, or without definite signification.

Bentham struggles with this difficulty, and arrives at two different solutions of the problem, both evidently untenable. One of these is based upon the apparent analogy between the state or community, and the natural man ; that is, he conceives the state as an actual being, susceptible like a man to pleasure and pain, and of being compensated for pain in one part by pleasure in another.

"That which is conformable to the utility or to the interest of an individual," he says, "is that which tends to augment the total sum of his happiness. That which is conformable to the utility or interest of the community, is that which tends to augment the total sum of the happiness of the individuals who compose it." Or, as Mr. Bain states, he defines utility as "the tendency of actions to promote the happiness and prevent the misery of the party under consideration; which party is usually the community in which one's lot is cast." But Mr. Bain's mode of stating the proposition is obviously a mere attempt to cover up the difficulty with words; for, as we have observed, there cannot be such a thing as happiness or welfare, except as existing in actual, sentient beings ; and there cannot, therefore, be a happiness or welfare of the community distinct from that of individuals.

Bentham's proposition, viz: that the welfare or happiness of a community is "the total sum of happiness of the individuals who compose it," is a little less indefinite, but hardly less objectionable. It, in effect, regards happiness in the abstract, without considering in whom it may exist, or the proportions in which it may be shared. Accordingly, he gives specific rules for calculating utility, which are the same in the case of a community as in that of the individual—the process being to calculate, by what he calls a process of moral arithmetic, on the one hand

all the pleasures, and on the other all the pains, which a
given act or class of acts may have a tendency to produce, and to strike a balance between them. Similarly
in the case of the state, if all the pleasures are experienced
by one set of individuals and all the pains by another, the
rule will still apply; and if the pleasures of the one set
are greater than the pains of the other, the act or class of
acts will be useful. Hence, it may even happen, considering the difference of men's sensibility to pleasant or un-
pleasant impressions, that the pleasures experienced by a
minority may be greater than the pains experienced by a
majority; and in such case the act or class of acts, according to the definition, will be useful and therefore
right—a theory obviously absurd, but so consonant to
human infirmity as to be unconsciously very generally
acted upon.

This is the theory of Bentham, as given in "The Theory
of Legislation." He seems, however, not to have been
satisfied with it; and at all events makes another effort
to solve the difficulty, and arrives at another and altogether different solution. This is, that the happiness or
interest of the majority must govern—a theory already
asserted by Hutcheson, Beccarria, and Priestly, the last of
whom he says "was the first (unless it was Beccarria)
who taught my lips to pronounce this sacred truth, that
the greatest happiness of the greatest number is the foundation of morals and legislation." But this may be fairly
called an execrable maxim; for it cannot be asserted that
the advantage of any number of men is a sufficient justifi-
cation for the infliction of an injury, even upon one innocent individual. There may indeed be exceptional cases,
in which the safety of the state or of a community may
absolutely require the sacrifice of the individual, and it
may be the duty of the individual to submit to this sacrifice, and the right of the state to require it; but the general principle must always obtain, that every man's life
and person are his own, and cannot, unless by virtue of
some clearly defined right, be converted to the use of another man, or of any number of men. To assert that any
innocent man's property or his person may be rightfully
violated, or any hurt done to him, whenever the advantage
of an undefined majority can be secured thereby, is a
proposition too shocking to the conscience and to the intelligence of mankind to require discussion.

§ 2. The most approved exponent of the doctrine of

utility in modern times is Mr. Mill, to whose views we have already briefly referred. As we have seen, he repudiates altogether the doctrine of individual or private utility; and hence, consistently enough, allows of the idea of duty and even of the most supreme self-devotion. But a still more singular emendation made by him of Bentham's theory is the following:

"That first of judicial virtues, impartiality, is an obligation of justice. * * * Society should treat all equally well who deserve equally well of it * * * this great moral duty being a direct emanation from the first principles of morals. * * * It is involved in the very meaning of utility, or the greatest .happiness principle. That principle is a mere form of words, without rational signification, unless one person's happiness, supposed equal in degree, * * * is counted for exactly as much as another's. These conditions being supplied, Bentham's dictum, ' Everybody to count for one, nobody for more than one,' might be written under the principle of utility, as an explanatory commentary."

But this gives to Bentham credit which he by no means deserves. He may, indeed, in portions of his work, have illogically made use of this, as well as other familiar principles, but it does not form a part of his theory, nor is it consistent with it. For, according to his fundamental principle, nobody's interest is counted except that of the individual affected. Nor is the proposition consistent even with the theory of general utility illegitimately assumed by Bentham; for, as we have seen, the two forms of this theory, as stated by him assert—the one, that the greatest amount of happiness is the standard, without regard to the individuals whose happiness is affected; and the other, that the happiness of the majority is the standard.

If, indeed, this principle of equality of value in the moral and jural claims of men can be assumed, as unquestionably it may be, then we have no further use of the theory of general utility. For this principle, as has been admirably shown by Mr. Spencer and others, is itself a sufficient foundation, at least, for the theory of justice. Hence, the theory of Mill cannot properly be called, as it has been, even "sublimated Benthamism." It is, in fact, a theory altogether different, and antagonistic to it.

As thus amended, the theory is morally unobjectionable; its defect,—if such a charge may be made against

so celebrated a logician as the **author,—is** want of logic.
Like Bentham and Austin, **and** other utilitarians, Mill
has failed to perceive that the **term** "*general utility*"
is absolutely without definite significance, and, therefore,
cannot serve as a sufficient premise for any theory. Accordingly, he uses the term in various senses; in **one,**
which I have quoted, he asserts that the standard **is "the
greatest** amount of happiness altogether," **thus seeming
to** agree with Bentham, in his first statement **of the**
theory; according to which it **is the greatest amount of**
happiness that can **be secured, even though that should**
be of **the** minority; but elsewhere he **says, "that the**
utilitarian's ideal of what is right is, not the agent's **own**
happiness, but that of all concerned"; or, in other words,
"the good of the **whole."** But this is an altogether different proposition, not **only from that** of individual, but
also from that of general utility, **and in nowise** different
from what is admitted by all moralists, **viz.:** that utility,
or tendency to promote the happiness **of** mankind, is, if
not of the essence, at least a property **of** right, and therefore universally **to** be predicated of it; or, **to** state the
proposition **in** a form more practically **useful, that no**
class of **acts** which, in their general consequences are **per-**
nicious, or contrary to the welfare **of** any **man, can be**
right. In **this** negative form, the principle of utility is
entirely unobjectionable, and **must be** accepted by all.

It is, therefore, obvious that utilitarianism is **merely**
another instance of error resulting from the use of **unde-**
fined, ambiguous, and nonsensical **terms; and** our observations on this head may **be closed by** adverting **to the**
fact that this is true with regard to **nearly** all the moral
and political speculations of the day, and by the further
observation that the pressing need, in **the** subject we are
discussing, as well as in others, is, not so much the acquisition **of** new knowledge, as to **get rid of the** false
semblance **of** knowledge which almost wholly **usurps the**
place of the true science, and thus **prevents all rational**
speculation.

CHAPTER VIII.

OF THE TRUE NATURE OF THE LAW AND OF RIGHTS.

§ 1. In the preceding chapters of this work our attention has been devoted to a critical examination of Austin's theory of jurisprudence, with a view of observing its inconsistencies, and the absurd consequences involved in it. To complete our view of the subject, the remaining chapter will be devoted to a brief statement of the antagonistic theory, referred to in our introductory chapter as the Common Law Doctrine, and elsewhere as the *Jural* Theory of the law; and to a cursory, but I trust sufficient, consideration of the principal arguments for and against it.

This theory, as there stated, rests upon the proposition that it is the function of government to establish justice, or to secure the observance of rights; and from this proposition,—if we define the law as including all the rules and principles by which the Courts are governed in determining controversies between men as to their mutual rights,—it follows that justice, or right,—which, as we have observed, is but the aggregate of the principles by which rights are determined,—is an integral part of the law; or, more specifically, of the law of Private Right, (*Jus Privatum;*) which constitutes the principal or *substantive* part of the law, and the only part that it is here material to consider, and which consists wholly of the doctrine of *rights*, and that of *actions.*

But rights also constitute one of the principal topics of Morality, and Right or Justice, one of the principal departments or divisions of that science. Hence, if the terms are in both cases used in the same sense, it follows that the doctrine of rights, or of Right or Justice, is a province common at once to the Law and to Morality; and, as is well observed by Mr. Amos, that "the term *rights* is the central term at once of the Science of Law, and of the Science of Morality." (The Science of Law, 88–89.)

The principal question involved in this discussion is, therefore, to determine whether the rights with which the law deals are rights in the proper sense, and therefore the same as those treated of in Morality, or whether—as is claimed by the *legists*,—they are something of an essentially different nature.

The latter proposition has been considered exhaustively, and it has been shown that the use of the term rights, and of the terms, Right or Justice, in the sense attributed to them by Austin and his followers, is unwarranted by correct usage, and that they stand absolutely alone in thus using them. It is now proposed to show affirmatively that the rights treated of in the law are rights, in the proper and ordinary sense of the term, and the identical rights treated of by moralists; and, hence,—as above asserted,—that Justice or Right is, in the same sense, at once a part of the law of Private Right, and a department or branch of Morality.

The arguments for this proposition will be drawn (1) from the significance of the terms, right and rights, and related terms, as determined by uniform and approved usage, and from the authority of jurists and philosophers, and of the law itself ; (2) from the historical development of the law ; (3) from an actual examination of the rights recognized in the law, or, as they are called, *juridical* rights ; and (4) from a consideration of the nature of jurisprudence, or the science of rights: after which, in conclusion, we will consider the principal objections that have been urged against this view.

§ 2. (1) The term, *a right*, or *rights*, and its numerous related terms,—such as *jurisdiction, judicial, courts of justice, the administration of justice, equity, good conscience, reason*, etc.,—all of which imply that the function of government is to administer *justice*, or to cause rights to be observed, are obviously used in the law in their ordinary and proper sense, as may be verified by reference to the following passages taken from approved authorities, and which might be indefinitely added to.

"The Common Law of England is the common rule for administering justice within this kingdom, and it asserts the royal prerogatives as well as the rights and liberties of the subject ";[1] hence, jurisdiction is defined as "an authority or power which a man has to do justice in causes of complaint brought before him."[2]

"It is to be observed," says Coke, "that the Common

[1] Sir Matthew Hale, cited, Jacob's Law Dic., " Common Law."
[2] Id. " Jurisdiction."

6

Law of England is sometimes called right, sometimes
common right, sometimes *communis justitia*. In the Great
Charter the Common Law is called Right. *Nulli vendimus,
nulli negabimus, aut differemus justitiam vel rectum.*"
" In the statute Wm. I., C. 1, it is called Common *Droit.
En primes voet le roy et commande * * * que common droit soit fait a touts, aussi bien a poers come aux
riches, sauns regard a nullay.* * * And Fleta
saith: " Quod communis justitia singulis puriter exhib-
eatur.*" And all the commissions and charters for execu-
tion of justice are *facturi quod ad justitiam pertinet se-
cundem legem et consuetudinem Angliæ.*"[1]

So it is explicitly asserted by Coke, that " the law of
Nature is part of the law of England"; and "this," he
says, " appeareth plainly and plentifully in our books."[2]

And the same proposition is explicitly asserted and explained at length by Fortescue, in the " De Laudibus Le-
gum Angliæ," and by St. Germain in " Doctor and Student."

The notion is also expressed by Coke in his celebrated
saying that, " *nihil quod est contra rationem est licitum,*"
and that " the common law itself is nothing else but reason" (Co.-Lit. 976); and in the more accurate definition
of Lord Mansfield, that the law is nothing else but reason
modified by habit and authority; and in the assertion of
Burke, that it is " the collected reason of ages, combining
the principles of original justice with the infinite variety of
human affairs"; and generally in all except the most recent of the text-books and reports.[3]

The notion of natural rights and justice, and that their
observance is the end of the law, is thus embodied in our
most familiar language, and has come to be a common
heritage of the race, of which it cannot be robbed by all
the assaults of a vain philosophy. It has, in fact, constituted the animating principle of progress in human civilization. Whatever has been gained in rational liberty,
in a better political organization, and in the greater security of life, liberty and property, is, in fact, due to
those who, by Bentham, are contemptuously called " fanatics armed with natural rights," and by Austin, " igno-

[1] Co.-Lit. 142a.
[2] Calvin's Case, 7 Coke's R. 12, 13.
[3] Bonham's Case, 8, Coke's Rep. 118 ; Hobart, 87 ; Bishop's First Book
of the Law, C. 9, § 90; Forbes vs. Cochvam. 2 Barn & Cres. 471; Coggs
vs. Bernard, 2 Lo. Raym. 911; Pasley vs. Freeman, 3 T. R 62; Millar
vs. Taylor, 4 Burr. 2312; O'Mychum vs. Barker, 1 Atk. 46; Davis vs.
Rowell Wills, 48-51; Lyle vs. Richards, 9 G. & R. 351.

rant and brawling fanatics, **who** stun you **with** their
pother about liberty." For **the** principle of justice,
though suppressed by the prevailing philosophy, **is, in**
fact, not only the fundamental truth of jural, and **of all**
political, and social science, but also the practical weapon
by which men have fought out their political emancipa-
tion.

§ 3. (2)[1] The nature of the development of the law has
been much misunderstood by the more **recent** English
jurists; and this misunderstanding, like others to which
I have alluded, is also the result of a failure to **distinguish**
between the different parts of the law. **Right or justice**
is **not** susceptible of development in any other sense **than**
in the sense in which the truths of mathematics and **other**
sciences may **be** said to be developed; **that is to say, they**
may be gradually discovered, but the **development is in**
our knowledge only. But it is otherwise **with the law of**
actions, which is, in fact, gradually developed, in **the**
sense that it is actually brought into being. Hence, con-
fining our attention to the Law of Private Right, the historical development of the law consists wholly in the development, not of rights, but of actions, or means of
enforcing rights. For right itself, or justice, is the same
at one period as another, and is at all **times** an integral
part of the law.[2]

In its essential features the **development of the law has**
been the same in the case of our own, and **in that of the**
Roman law; and from this, and our knowledge of human
nature generally, it may be assumed **that** it is governed
by general laws, which, under similar **circumstances, will**
always produce essentially identical **results.**

These results may be stated **with substantial accuracy**
as follows:

Every **system of** positive **law commences with the mere**
establishment of **a** jurisdiction, **or power to administer**

[1] The subject of this and the following sections **is treated of** more at
length in "Right and Law," and in "The Law **of Private** Right,"
cited *supra*; to which the reader, if he desires to **pursue the** subject
further, is requested to refer.

[2] "The principles of natural right (*naturalia jura*,) which are observed
equally by all peoples, being established, as it were, by Divine Provi-
dence, remain always firm and immutable; but those which each state
has established for itself are often changed, either by tacit consent of
the people or by some later law." (Pandects.)
And to the same effect it is said of our own law by Coke:
"*Leges naturæ*," (*naturalia jura*,) "*perfectissimæ sunt et immutabiles;
humani vero juris conditio semper in infinitum currit, et nihil est in eo quod
perpetuo stare possit; leges humanæ nascuntur vivunt et moriuntur.*" Calvin's Case, 7 Coke's R. 25.

justice; which is at first generally vested in a king or monarch, but afterwards delegated to regular courts for the administration of justice. At this period justice, or Natural Right, constitutes the whole law of the state.

From this beginning, the law of private right, or rather the law of actions,—which, as we have observed, is alone capable of development,—is developed by the courts, in the main without legislative interference; and its development,—with the exception of a few statutory provisions,—is the result of the exercise of *jurisdiction,* and not of legislative power; and hence the law of private right is to be regarded as an expression of the judgment, not of the will of the state.

The exercise of jurisdiction,—*ex vi termini,*—consists merely in devising appropriate remedies, or actions for recognized rights; and in the performance of this function the Courts, and more especially the Courts of Equity, have, in the main, avowedly governed themselves, in the determination of cases, by the principles of justice, or natural right. Hence, every step in the development of the law, (if we leave out of view the comparatively limited influence of statutory legislation,) has consisted in the application, or attempted application, of principles of natural right to cases actually presented; and hence, in theory, and, so far forth as the functions of the Courts have been well performed, in fact also, the law of actions is but a practical application of the principles of right.

The fact that the principles of natural right, or most of its principles, are, and for a long time have been, recognized by the Courts, and some, of course, by the Legislature, is not inconsistent with the proposition that they still continue to be principles of natural right; but, on the contrary, constitutes the most conclusive proof of their truth. For it may be asserted as a universal proposition, that in a progressive civilization no principal can endure in the law if inconsistent with justice. Thus, the *jus civile* of every system, that is, the portion of the law that is arbitrary and peculiar, though commonly supposed by modern English jurists to be immutable, except by legislation, is, in fact, as Coke asserts, the mutable and temporary part of the law; while the part of it which consists in Right or Justice is alone permanent and immutable. Hence, if we compare the law as it existed in the time of Edward I., or even at a much later period, with the law as it exists today, or, if we compare the law,—as opposed to Equity,—as it was at the time of Blackstone, with the present law, we find there is hardly anything common between them except the principles of natural right recognized from the earliest times, throughout all stages of the law, to the present day.

The process of development has been the same in the Roman as in our own law, but the former has come to an end, while ours remains, it is hoped, to be the subject of a further and higher development. Such development, however, will not consist in contemning and rejecting the methods by which such noble results were obtained by the Roman lawyers ; or in rejecting the moral convictions and moral faith, to which is owing the present European civilization ; nor in the attempt to substitute for the principles of natural right the arbitrary enactments of codes : but in more consistently recognizing the sacredness of rights and of justice, and in the logical development of the principles of Natural Right, as established in the common moral convictions or conscience of the civilized world.

§ 4. (3) A mere enumeration of the rights recognized in the law will be sufficient to show that they are none other than those *natural* or *moral* rights,—so despised by the legists,—which are recognized universally by the people.

These rights are of two general classes, namely, rights of *ownership* and rights of *obligation*. Under the former head are included the right of property, the right of personal liberty or of self-ownership, and the right of husband in wife, and parent in child, etc., and *vice versa ;* under the latter, the right to the performance of contracts, the right to restitution or compensation for injuries, and certain rights which arise *ex mero jure,* without the intervention of contract or delict,—as, for example, the right of salvage in case of a derelict ship. The last class is a limited one, and may be left out of view in the present connection ; it is mentioned merely to make our enumeration complete.

The above classification covers all rights, juridical or non-juridical, and it is evident that they are all recognized at once by the law and by the people generally. Hence, it is clear, a juridical right is nothing more than a *natural* or *moral* right, with an action or remedy provided for it by law ; and that the law itself, "in principle at least," is merely "justice armed with force." (Cousin, The True, the Beautiful, and the Good, Lecture 15.)

These rights are recognized in all systems of law, and in

all civilized countries they are efficiently protected; and, in fact, the civilization of every country is to be judged by the more or less effectual manner in which this is the case. Hence, juridical rights are obviously the same throughout the civilized world; and a man may travel anywhere without finding that he has a different set of rights in one country from what he has in another. Everywhere, for instance, he will find his right to his watch, to his personal apparel or other property, to the repayment of a loan, or to the performance of any other contract, or to restitution or compensation for injury,—in short, nearly every right he has at home equally recognized and enforced.

Hence, it is evident, in every country the doctrine of rights is part of the law of private right, and this part of the law is everywhere the same. And thus far the noble prophecy of Cicero is in fact realized: " *Non erit alia lex Romæ, alia Athenis ; alia nunc, alia posthac ; sed et apud omnes gentes, et omnia tempora una eademque lex obtinebit.*"

§ 5. (4) Jurisprudence we have defined as the Science, or, more accurately, the Science and the Art of Justice, or of Rights. It is its fundamenta characteristic that it deals, not with *actual*, but with *rightful* powers, or rights ; and that its fundamental problem is to determine, not the historical question as to what powers men, either as individuals, or collectively as the state, may actually have, at any particular time or place, but the theoretical question as to the powers which either individuals or the state ought to have, either in general, or under given circumstances of time and place.

This, with reference to theoretical jurisprudence, is sufficiently obvious; but the proposition is equally true, though not so apparent, with reference to practical jurisprudence. For no fact is more certain, though obscured in this country and England by the prevailing philosphy, than that it is the function or duty of the state to administer, or, (in the language of the Constitution of the United States) to " establish justice," and that this duty, and consequently justice or natural right, are universally recognized by civilized states.

That this duty should be imperfectly realized is simply due to the necessary and inevitable imperfection of all human instrumentality ; and from this fact arise numerous difficulties and apparent objections, which will hereafter be considered. But, for the present, we will assume the view of the nature of jurisprudence above given to be correct, and will proceed to show that it is confirmed by a more detailed examination of the subject.

As the term "a right" includes in its signification, or connotes, the idea of rightness, it would seem to be necessary in order to render our definition of rights complete, to define the adjective "right," or the term "right," as used to denote a quality ; but to do this would involve the solution of the metaphysical problem as to the nature of right and duty,—a question about which theories widely differ, and which, in the present state of ethical science, cannot, perhaps, be satisfactorily solved ; and which is, in fact, the rock upon which the English jurists have been wrecked. But this, indeed, is a problem which it is unnecessary for us to consider ; for it is manifestly indifferent what theory be adopted, provided only that it asserts the reality of moral distinctions.

It may, however, be fairly asked : By what standard or test are right and wrong to be judged ? And this is a question that must be answered. The answer to it is that there are, in fact, two standards, intimately related to each other, but which yet must be distinguished ; namely, the practical, and the theoretical standard,—the former being the standard by which our conduct, in matters affecting others, is to be governed ; the latter, the standard by which our judgments are to be formed.

In matters that concern ourselves alone, these two standards coincide ; for to every man the practical test of right and wrong must be his own conscience, or moral convictions. But in matters of common concern it is otherwise, and for such cases another standard must be sought ; and this can be no other than the common moral convictions, or general conscience of the people.

The nature of this *consensus* of moral conviction, or general conscience of the people, the method of its genesis, its rightful authority, and the instrumentality by which it is enforced,—which is public opinion,—is a subject of fundamental importance in jurisprudence, and in politics generally, but is too extensive to permit of discussion here. But it may be asserted, as a fact which the reader can verify for himself, that this general conscience of civilized men, or, in other words, positive morality, ought to be, and, in fact, ultimately and in the long run is, the paramount predominating political force in the civilized world, and that it is this that makes civilization possible ;

and also that the superior development of this force in modern civilization constitutes the essential difference by which it is to be distinguished from that of the ancient world, and other less advanced civilizations.

Nor can it be doubted, either that this is, or that it ought to be, the practical test or standard, in all matters of common concern; and this for three reasons. For, first, the positive morality of the present age is the result of the never-ending struggle of mankind to realize theoretical morality,—a struggle to which, from the beginning of history, the highest intellect and conscience of the race have been consecrated,—and it therefore carries with it the strongest presumption of its truth; secondly, there is no alternative between the acceptance of this standard, and submission to arbitrary power, and hence free government is possible only to the extent that this general conscience is developed; and thirdly, men, as it were by some instinct of their nature, in fact accept and submit to this test as the true standard of practical morality; for, as is well observed by Mill, "the customary morality,— that which education and opinion have consecrated,—is the only one that presents itself to the mind with the feeling of being, *in itself*, obligatory."[1]

It is, however, evident, in view of the difference in the morality of different peoples and ages, and of different classes and individuals in the same age and country,—a difference that really exists, though greatly exaggerated, —that positive morality cannot be accepted as infallible; and for this the reason is very apparent. Morality depends upon a few fundamental principles, from which its subordinate principles and rules may be logically deduced; but, as Hobbes observes, the generality of men are so far from being capable of consistently applying the rules of logic, "that they know not what it is." Hence, while all men reason to a certain extent, they do not reason consistently; and thus, in practical matters, their only safe guide is experience; by which their notions are constantly corrected. Thus, in the main, in practical results, positive coincides with theoretical morality; but it differs from it in this, that it consists of rules rather than of principles; and that these rules are deduced, not by accurate logical deduction from principles, but by a rough kind of induction or experiment. From which it results that the rules themselves are not accurately formu-

[1] Utilitarianism, Ch. 3, pp. 38, 39.

lated, but are made to conform to truth only by the aid of numerous exceptions, and hence are logically unserviceable. On the other hand, scientific morality accepts no proposition except as universally true, both immediately and in all its logical consequences, and admits no conclusions except such as can be rigidly demonstrated from the principles assumed. It is, therefore, a true deductive science, as certain in its method and in its results as Geometry, or, to take a more nearly related instance, Political Economy.

It is, however, always to be remembered that the principles of scientific morality, though conclusive on the conscience of him who is convinced, cannot become practically operative as a common rule or standard of right and wrong, until they meet with general acceptance, and become established in the general conscience, or common moral convictions of the people. And hence, the practical end of scientific jurisprudence, in relation to matters of common concern, is to enlighten the general conscience, and to correct and reform the moral convictions of mankind. To use the striking metaphor of Pindar, *Nomos* alone is King, and the function of Philosophy is only to advise.

Of the possibility of a scientific morality there cannot be any reasonable doubt; and I therefore say, with Locke: "Confident I am that if men would, in the same method and with the same indifferency, search after moral as they do after mathematical truths, they would find them to have a stronger connection one with another, and a more necessary consequence from our clear and distinct ideas, and to come nearer perfect demonstration, than is commonly imagined." And this is peculiarly and in the highest degree true of Jurisprudence, or the Science of Rights. For this science rests upon a few simple fundamental principles, about which there is not, and cannot be, any dispute.

Of these the principal are the following:

(1) The first is the conclusion reached in our review of Hobbes' theory of Rights, to which, in order to avoid repetition, the reader is requested to turn: it is, that *the rightful or jural liberty of the individual is limited, and limited only, by the rights of other individuals or the State.*

(2) To this is to be added the obvious principle, that *there is always a presumption in favor of liberty*, and,

hence, *where a right is asserted, either in an individual or in the State, that derogates from the liberty of another, the burden of proof is on him who asserts the existence of the right.*

(3) From this it follows that *the existence of a right in any one, derogating from the liberty of another, cannot be affirmed, unless it can be equally affirmed of all others standing in similar jural relations ;* for the burden of proof rests upon him who asserts the right, and, according to the hypothesis, no reason can be assigned why such a right should exist in one, which would not, in a like case, exist in another.

Or, the proposition may be otherwise stated, by saying that *the jural liberty of all men, in the same case, is equal,*—meaning by the term, " *the same case,*" a similarity of all circumstances material to the question of right.

(4) It is an obvious consequence from the nature of a right, that *one who has been unjustly deprived of its exercise should be restored to its enjoyment ;* and it seems equally obvious, that *where restitution in kind is impracticable, restitution in value, or compensation, should be made.*

(5) To the above is to be added the principle of utility, in the negative form, in which it has been stated, viz, that *whatever can be shown to be, in its general consequences, pernicious or detrimental to mankind, is wrong.*

This principle is embodied, under the name of the *argumentum ab inconvenienti,* in one of the fundamental maxims of our law ; and there are few principles more frequently referred to and relied upon by jurists than this. The maxim, as given by Coke, is *Argumentum ab inconvenienti plurimum valet in lege ;* and he adds : " The law, that is, the perfection of reason, cannot suffer anything that is inconvenient ; and therefore he says : " *Nihil quod est inconveniens est licium* " ; and that " judges are to judge of inconveniences as of things unlawful."

(6) *But in considering the question of inconvenience, regard must be had, not to particular, but to general consequences ; or, in other words, not to the effect of the decision in the particular case under consideration, but to its effect as a precedent or rule.* For what is right or wrong, just or unjust, in any case must necessarily be so in other like cases ; and *hence right, as well as morality generally, must consist of general rules applying to all cases of the same class.* This is insisted upon by all mor-

alists, and is but a statement of Kant's Categorical Imperative.

All of the above principles are, in fact, assumed in our **law**, and also in the Roman law ; and the doctrine of Rights, as established in both systems, and in all systems, is, in the main, deduced from them.[1]

There does not seem to be any room for difference of opinion with regard to these principles ; and hence **all** disagreement, as to the subordinate principles of right, must be regarded as resulting wholly from defects in the logic of one, **or the** other, or both, of **the** parties differing. If jurists, instead of losing themselves in metaphysical abstractions as to the nature of moral distinctions, would accept, as sufficiently verified, the fundamental principles of justice, assumed in all systems of law, and would address themselves to the task of applying to them **the** logical method, and of thus reducing to logical consistency the received principles of right, which have been with more or less consistency derived from these fundamental principles, it cannot be doubted that a substantially perfect unanimity could be reached, or that the law would thus be perfected. But, unfortunately, it is one of the worst vices of the *legal* theory, that it seeks to banish from the law **Logic, or** Reason, as well as Justice.

§ 6. There are numerous, and apparently formidable objections to the above views, **as** to **the** nature **of the** law and of jurisprudence ; but these are apparent only, and a consideration of them will serve rather to confirm our theory than to raise any doubt as to its correctness.

(1) Until comparatively recent times the close **connec-tion**, or rather, to the extent explained above, the identity, of morality with the law was generally recognized by jurists; who accordingly regarded the one, as well as the **other, as** belonging to their province, **and were** equally familiar with both. But this, unfortunately, is no longer true, at least in England ; **for, in** fact, **so** far **as we may** judge from their published utterances, there is no other class of **men** who care **or know so** little about Moral Science as the modern English jurists; **for, with** regard to it, they do not merely participate **in the** general disregard and neglect into which it **has fallen** with other peo-

[1] I have elsewhere attempted to show this in detail. Right and **Law,** Book I : The Law of Private Right, Part III.

It has also, as we have observed, been shown, on the whole successfully, by Herbert Spencer, in " Social Statistics," and in "Justice"; and by Kant in the " Philosophy of Right."

ple, but regard it with affirmative dislike, as a delusion peculiarly pernicious to jurisprudence, and as indicating certain tendencies of human nature, which, like original sin, must be rooted out, before jural or political salvation can be hoped for. Hence has originated the feeling that there is some great and mysterious danger to be apprehended from admitting that the law has any connection with justice, or morality.

But this objection is obviously based on the failure to apprehend, or to observe, the essential distinction between justice, and the rest of morality. The law does not pretend to enforce morality, generally, but to enforce that part of it only which morality demands shall be enforced, namely, justice or right. With the duties of charity and benevolence generally the State does not,—or, at least, need not,—concern itself; but the observance of justice is at once the end of government, and the condition of its permanence.

(2) A more serious objection is that the law of private right, and even the part of it that treats of rights, is, to some extent, made up of laws and statutes, and, to a still larger extent, of customs; and there is an apparent difficulty in reconciling with our theory the existence of these elements; of which the one is accidental in its nature, and the other arbitrary.

There is, indeed, no difficulty in reconciling the co-existence of these three elements in the law, if we regard them simply as co-ordinate: but our theory asserts the paramount authority of justice or right in that part of the law of private right which treats of rights; and that neither statutes nor customs are co-ordinate and independent parts of right; and this proposition is apparently more difficult to accept.

The objection, however, is more apparent than real. Laws or statutes are mere acts of men, differing from other men only in being clothed with the power or right of legislation. Generically, they are of essentially the same nature as contracts, grants, and other expressions of human will, which, like laws, are valid or otherwise, according to the right of the party making them. Hence, when it is within the right of the legislator to determine any matter, the expression of its will with regard to it is conclusive; and rights may, therefore, originate in legislation precisely as in contract, or delict, which the moralist, as well as the lawyer, must recognize. But if the law is in excess of the rightful power of the legislator, or, to use a technical expression, is *ultra vires*, it has no more force or validity than the act of a private individual, which is beyond his right.

Hence, the existence or non-existence of rights cannot be predicated from the mere enactment of a law, but their validity must depend upon the existence of a precedent right in the state. And this is true, whatever theory be adopted as to the extent of that right. For, even if it could be assumed that the right of the state is absolute, this could only be on the ground that this is a principle of reason or natural right; and a right created by a law would still be a true right, or, as we may call it,—precisely as a right created by contract or grant—a natural right.

Laws or statutes, therefore, do not enter into Right otherwise than as mere elements in the problem of determining rights; and their validity and effect must ultimately be determined by some principle of natural right, even if it should be none other than that the right or power of the state over the lives and fortunes of its subjects is absolute.

With regard to custom, the case, *mutatis mutandis*, is the same. A custom may or may not give rise to a right, and whether it does so or not is a question to be determined by some principle of reason or natural right. Thus obviously, on principles of natural reason, custom enters into and forms part of contracts, and is also an important element in the determination of rights arising from delict; and it otherwise—and this is its most important aspect,—often has the force of law. To explain why this is the case would be to enter into too large a subject to be treated here, but it is admitted that custom, in order to be law, must be reasonable, and its effect, therefore, like that of laws, is to be determined by principles of reason or natural right. Hence, like laws or statutes, customs do not of themselves originate rights, but only by virtue of the principles of Right, and they therefore enter into the determination of rights merely as elements of the problem.

These observations directly apply also to precedents or judicial decisions, which, though entitled to respectful consideration as authority, are binding only when they enter into the general habits of the community, and thus become established by custom.

(3) It is a very common opinion, and if true a serious objection to our theory, that the courts do not and cannot

determine questions of right by the principles of abstract
justice alone. They are in many cases, it is said, prevented from doing so by some positive rule, either enacted
by the legislature or established by precedent. But this
objection, like others, arises from the habit already referred to of looking at the law as a homogeneous whole
instead of distinguishing its separate parts. In questions
of procedure, the judge may often be unable to do justice. He may, for instance, be prevented from doing it
by want of power or jurisdiction; or, he may even be
compelled, or at least judges often think themselves compelled, to do an act of injustice,—though this is more generally the fault of the judge than of the law. So, too, in
determining the practical question of action or no action,
he may be prevented by the arbitrary or accidental rules
of the law from doing justice. But in determining the
question of Right, neither judicial nor legislative authority
is of any weight except as a mere element in the problem,
but precisely the same problem is presented to the jurist
as to the moralist, namely : in view of all the elements of
the case, including statutes and customs, if they bear upon
it, to determine the simple question of right or justice presented, which from its nature can be determined only by
principles of natural right or reason ; nor is there a conceivable case in which he will be justified in looking upon
the question in any other light.

Whether when the right shall be determined there will
be a corresponding action or not, is another question,
and one on which statutes and precedents may exert more
or less influence ; but the two questions are altogether
distinct, and can only be confused at the expense of the
integrity of the intellect, and of the conscience of the
judge.

(4)   Hence, as the rule of decision in determining actions is, to some extent, different from that by which the
judge is to be guided in determining the mere question of
right, there must ensue in some cases a discrepancy in
results.   For while in theory actions should correspond
precisely with rights, in practice they fail to do so, and
thus many rights are without the corresponding remedy.
Hence, in practical jurisprudence, we have the distinction,
unknown to the theory of right, between actionable and
non-actionable, or, as they are otherwise called, between
juridical and non-juridical rights—a distinction in theory
extremely important to observe, and with reference to

practice no less so; for there is no fallacy more common,
or more pernicious in its consequences than to infer,
from the non-existence of an action or remedy, the non-
existence of the right.

But the contrary is not only an obvious and necessary
deduction from the very notion of right, but is very clearly
recognized in our law. Thus, it is a well-settled principle
that a right barred by the statute of limitations continues
to exist, though the remedy be forever gone. So, also, it
has been repeatedly held with reference to contracts declared void by the usury and banking acts, and with reference to conveyances of married women declared void by
statute on account of defective acknowledgments, and with
reference to marriages technically void for want of compliance with statutory provisions as to the mode of sol-
emnization,—that rights existed under and by virtue of
such contracts, conveyances, and marriages, though expressly declared to be void by statute; and accordingly,
subsequent statutes declaring them valid have been up-
held, on the ground that the validating acts did not create
new rights, but simply provided remedies for rights already existing. Otherwise such laws would be clearly
unconstitutional; for on the theory that there were no
pre-existing rights, they would operate to transfer the
property of one set of persons to another; which is forbidden by all the American Constitutions, State and Federal.[1]

The existence of non-actionable rights is also very fully
recognized, and many important consequences deduced
from it in the Roman and in modern Civil Law.[2]

The obvious distinction between *actionable* and *non-
actionable*, or *juridical* and *non juridical* rights, is not,
however, to be confounded with the distinction made by
Austin and his school, (heretofore alluded to,) between
legal and *moral* rights. The latter is altogether untenable; for, as we have already observed, the term a right
implies, as part of its essential signification, the quality of
rightness; and hence there can no more be a right that is
not a moral right than there can be a four-sided triangle
or a square circle.

[1] Sichel vs. Carillo, 42 Cal. 493; Syracuse Bank vs. Davis, 16 Barb. 103;
Dentzel vs. Waldie, 30 Cal. 144; Goshen vs. Stonington, 4 Conn. 309.
[2] Savigny on Obligations, Brown's Abridgement, §§ 5-11.

Finis.

www.ingramcontent.com/pod-product-compliance
Lightning Source LLC
Chambersburg PA
CBHW020256090426
42735CB00009B/1111